JEWISH HOLIDAY
CRAFTS
FOR LITTLE HANDS

Ruth Esrig Brinn
with Judyth Groner and Madeline Wikler

illustrated by
Katherine Janus Kahn

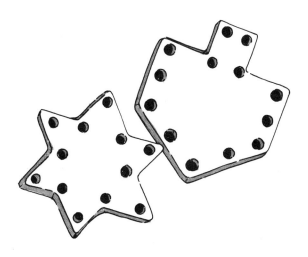

KAR-BEN COPIES, INC.   ROCKVILLE, MD

A NOTE TO PARENTS AND TEACHERS

Jewish Holiday Crafts for Little Hands is designed to help young children relate to, and feel part of each Jewish holiday or festival.

Materials used are mostly notions and scrap items found around the house. Remember to save old magazines, packing material, tissue paper, leftover wallpaper and fabric, empty spice jars, egg cartons, juice cans, spools, etc. Help children organize collection boxes of their own.

Candlesticks, a kiddush cup, flowers, and an attractive challah covering are the basic "ingredients" for most Jewish celebrations. This book gives several ways to make these items. Don't forget to use what your child creates. Crystal, china, and construction paper do indeed complement each other!

To the new generation, beginning with Lior Avraham,
Ayelet Rose, Ashira Liba, and T'hela Fei. . .

—R.E.B.

Library of Congress Cataloging-in-Publication Data

Brinn, Ruth Esrig.
    Jewish holiday crafts for little hands/Ruth Esrig Brinn; illustrated by Katherine Janus Kahn.
        p.   cm.
    Summary: Provides simple directions for making over 100 craft items from easily available materials for Shabbat and various Jewish holidays. Includes a glossary and summary of the holidays.
    ISBN 0-929371-47-X (pbk.):
    1. Jewish crafts—Juvenile literature. 2. Fasts and feasts—Judaism—Juvenile literature. (1. Jewish crafts. 2. Handicraft. 3. Fasts and feasts—Judaism.) I. Kahn, Katherine, ill. II. Title.
BM729.H35B74   1993
296.4'3—dc20

92-39638
CIP
AC

Text copyright © 1993 by Kar-Ben Copies, Inc.
Illustrations copyright © 1993 by Katherine Janus Kahn
All rights reserved. No portion of this book may be reproduced without the written permission of the publisher.
Published by KAR-BEN COPIES, INC., Rockville, MD 1-800-4-KARBEN
Printed in the United States of America.

_____

Some of these crafts have previously appeared in Let's Celebrate, More Let's Celebrate, *and* Let's Have A Party *by Ruth Esrig Brinn, and* My Very Own Jewish Calendar *by Judyth Groner and Madeline Wikler.*

CONTENTS

SHABBAT

When God finished creating the world, the heavens and the earth, the trees and flowers, the birds and the animals, man and woman, God created a day for rest, and called it Shabbat. Shabbat comes every week. It is a time of joy and family celebration. On Friday at sundown, we welcome Shabbat with the lighting of the candles. On Saturday at sunset, we say good-bye to Shabbat with the ceremony of Havdallah.

WORDS TO KNOW

Shabbat — Sabbath, day of rest

Tzedakah — contributions to charity and acts of kindness; the word means "justice"

Challah — braided Sabbath bread

Kiddush cup — wine cup

Havdallah — ceremony that ends Shabbat; the word means "separation." Havdallah includes blessings over wine, a braided candle, and spices.

SHABBAT

CANDLE AND FLOWER CENTERPIECE

What You Need:

Two long cardboard
  rolls (for candles)
One short cardboard
  roll (for vase)
Straws
Paper plate
Colored paper
Tissue paper
Scissors, glue

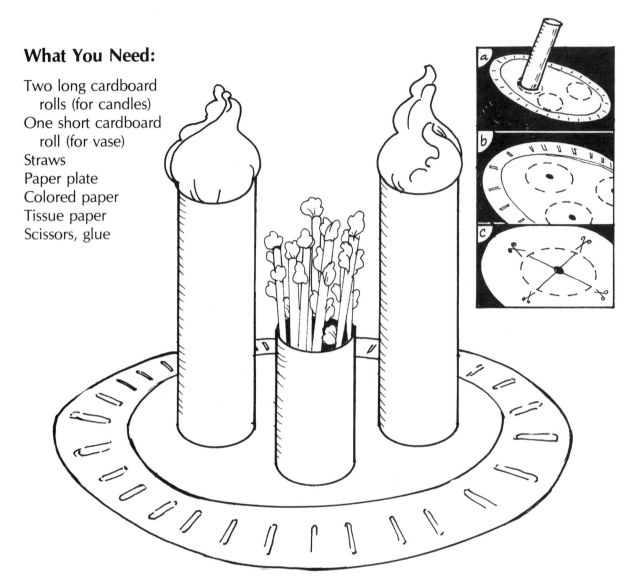

What You Do:

1. The paper plate will be the base for your centerpiece. Use the cardboard rolls to trace three circles on the back of the plate. Punch a small hole in the center of each circle and cut four slits from the hole to the circle's edge.

2. Cover the rolls with tissue or colored paper.

3. Push each of the rolls into one of the slit circles.

4. Stuff a crumpled tissue "flame" into the top of each candlestick.

5. Crumple small pieces of colored tissue, and glue onto straws. Put your flowers into the vase.

6

What You Need:

Coffee can or container with plastic lid
Aluminum foil or colored paper
Decorating scraps
Scissors, glue

What You Do:

1. Cover the container with foil or colored paper and decorate it with Shabbat designs. Make a slit in the lid.

2. Before Shabbat begins, drop a few coins into your tzedakah box.

A PAIR OF CANDLESTICKS

What You Need:

Six empty spools
Two small wooden blocks
Glue
Paint
Two metal bottle caps

What You Do:

1. For each candlestick, glue three spools together. Glue the spools to a block. Wait until the glue is very hard and dry.

2. Paint the candlesticks. Glue a metal bottle cap on top.

7

SHINE-THROUGH KIDDUSH CUP

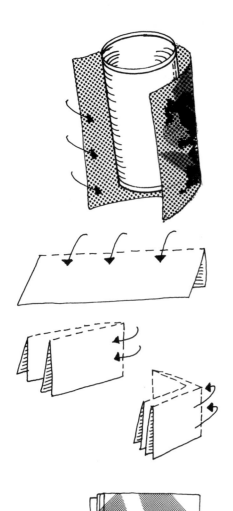

What You Need:

Orange juice can
Aluminum foil
Colored paper
Scissors, glue, markers

What You Do:

1. Cut a piece of foil large enough to wrap around the can. Scribble on the foil with different colored markers. Wrinkle up the foil and then smooth it out. Cover the can with the foil, tucking in the edges.

2. Cut a piece of colored paper that will fit around the can exactly. Fold it in half lengthwise. Then fold it in half the other way twice.

3. Cut shapes from the corners and from each side. Open the paper carefully. Roll it around the can and glue the edges together.

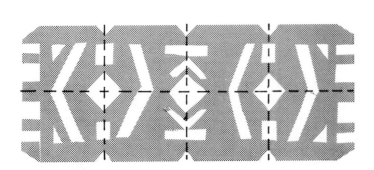

PAPIER MACHE KIDDUSH CUP

What You Need:

Flour and water
Orange juice can
Newspaper strips
Paper towel
Paint, glue

What You Do:

1. To make paste, mix together four tablespoons of flour and eight tablespoons of water.

2. Spread paste over the can and cover with a layer of newspaper strips. Do this three or four more times. On top of the last layer of paste, use a paper towel. Wait until your cup is dry and hard.

3. Paint the cup with Shabbat designs.

WINE COASTERS

What You Need:

Plastic lids (from margarine tubs or coffee cans)
Old holiday greeting cards
Clear adhesive-backed paper
Scissors, glue

What You Do:

1. Cut designs from the greeting cards, and glue them onto the inside of the plastic lid.

2. Using the lid as a guide, trace a circle on the backing of the adhesive paper. When you cut out the circle, cut it slightly smaller than the tracing.

3. Carefully remove the backing from the adhesive, and cover your design with the plastic to seal. Your wine coaster is ready for Shabbat.

TWO CHALLAH COVERS

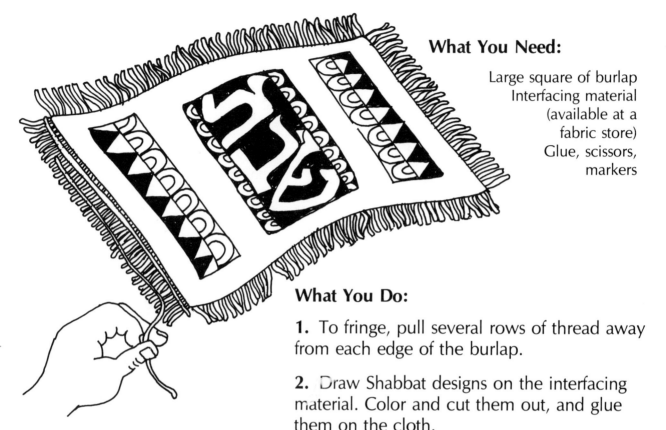

What You Need:

Large square of burlap
Interfacing material
(available at a
fabric store)
Glue, scissors,
markers

What You Do:

1. To fringe, pull several rows of thread away from each edge of the burlap.

2. Draw Shabbat designs on the interfacing material. Color and cut them out, and glue them on the cloth.

What You Need:

Large handkerchief or piece of
material
Crayons
Clean white paper
Iron

What You Do:

1. Draw fringes all around the edges of your cloth. Push hard with your crayons to make the colors show. Draw a Shabbat design in the center of the cloth or write the word "Challah."

2. Put the white paper over the cloth and iron. This will keep the colors bright.

SALT SHAKER FOR SHABBAT

What You Need:

3 empty spools
Aluminum foil
Pencil or straw
Button
Glue, tape
Salt

What You Do:

1. Glue the spools together in a stack. Push a straw or pencil through the holes to keep them straight while the glue is drying.

2. Glue a button over the top opening.

3. Turn over and fill with salt. Tape the bottom opening so the salt won't spill. Wrap foil around the spools.

What You Need:

Small paper bag
Crayons or paint
Glue
Newspaper
String

What You Do:

1. Color or paint the paper bag. Fold and glue down the corners.

2. Draw eyes on your fish. Stuff the bag with bits of newspaper and tie the open end to make a tail.

A RING OF FLOWERS

What You Need:

Colored construction paper
Colored tissue paper
Glue, scissors, markers

glue

What You Do:

1. Cut a long strip of colored paper about 2″ wide for the ring.

2. Cut several stems from green paper and glue them to the ring. The bottom of each stem should reach the bottom of the strip for support.

3. Cut flowers in different shapes and colors. Decorate with markers and tissue paper. Glue them to the stems.

4. Glue the edges of the strip together to make a ring.

SHABBAT CHARADES

Divide your guests into small groups of two or three. Give each group a note telling them what scene in Jewish history to dramatize. Let each team rehearse in a different part of the room or house. After five or ten minutes call everyone together, and let each group perform. See how long it takes to guess each charade. Here are some suggestions for scenes to enact:

- Adam and Eve in the Garden of Eden
- Noah Building the Ark
- Moses Leading the Jewish People Out of Egypt
- Abraham Smashing the Idols
- Joseph Interpreting Pharaoh's Dreams

- The Maccabees Finding the Jug of Oil and Rededicating the Temple
- Queen Esther Accusing Haman of his Plot to Kill the Jews
- Jonah in the Whale

HAVDALLAH HOUSE

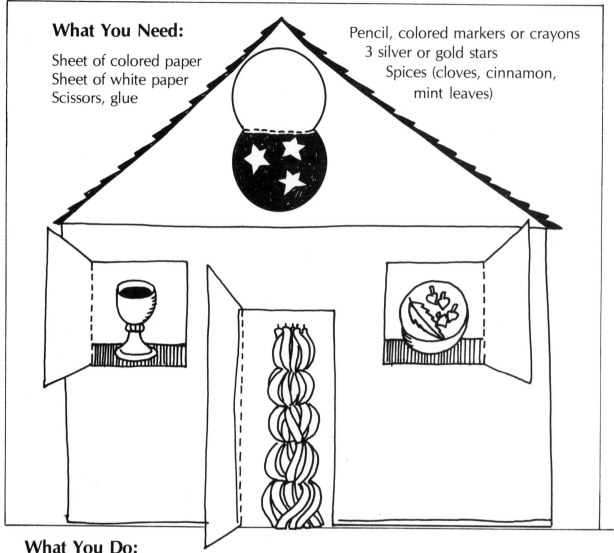

What You Need:

Sheet of colored paper
Sheet of white paper
Scissors, glue

Pencil, colored markers or crayons
3 silver or gold stars
Spices (cloves, cinnamon,
mint leaves)

What You Do:

1. Draw a simple house shape on the colored paper and cut it out.

2. Draw a large door, 2 square windows and a round attic window. (To make a round window, trace around the bottom of a juice glass.)

3. Carefully cut the door and windows on three sides. Fold back along the fourth side.

4. Glue the house to the white paper. Be careful not to glue the windows or door.

5. Draw a tall twisted Havdallah candle behind the tall door. Draw a cup of wine behind one square window. Draw a small bowl behind the other square window. Glue some spices on the bowl.

6. Color the attic window opening black, and stick on the three stars.

HAVDALLAH SPICE BOX OR JAR

What You Need:

Small jar, bottle, can, or box with lid
Colored paper or wrapping paper
Scissors, glue
Silver or gold stars
Whole cloves, mint leaves, or
    cinnamon stick pieces

What You Do:

1. Cover the jar or can with colored paper. Decorate the sides and lid with shiny stars.

2. Fill the jar with spices.

ROSH HASHANAH AND YOM KIPPUR

Tekiah! the shofar calls to us on Rosh Hashanah. A new year is beginning. It is a happy time. We celebrate with family and friends, and share apples and honey for a sweet new year. It is also a serious time. We pray that we can change and grow to make the new year even better than the last. For the ten days between Rosh Hashanah and Yom Kippur, we think about the year that has passed and the year that is to come. On Yom Kippur we fast and pray and ask forgiveness for the things we have done wrong. The shofar sounds again at the end of Yom Kippur, to mark a new beginning.

WORDS TO KNOW

Rosh Hashanah — New Year

Yom Kippur — Day of Forgiveness

Shanah Tovah—"A Good Year"

Shofar — ram's horn blown to welcome the new year

Challah — braided holiday bread. The Rosh Hashanah challah is round, like the cycle of the year.

Kiddush cup — wine cup

Yom Tov — holiday

ROSH HASHANAH

YOM KIPPUR

WHEEL OF TIME

What You Need:

Paper plate
Construction paper
Markers
Paper fastener

TISHRI/*Rosh Hashanah*
CHESHVAN
KISLEV/*Hanukkah*
TEVET
SHEVAT/*Tu B'Shevat*
ADAR/*Purim*
NISAN/*Passover*
IYAR/*Yom Ha'atzmaut*
SIVAN/*Shavuot*
TAMMUZ
AV
ELUL

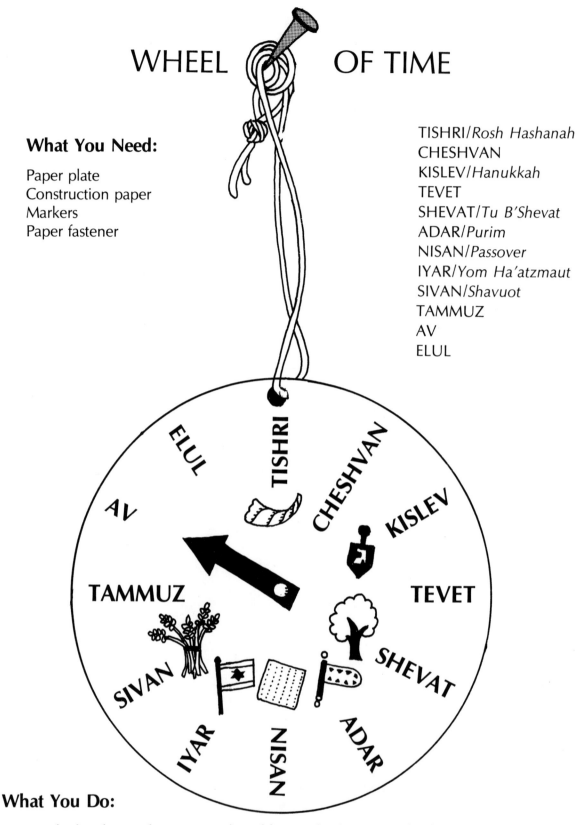

What You Do:

1. Mark the face of a paper plate like a clock. Instead of numbers, print the names of the Hebrew months. Draw holiday symbols at the appropriate months.

2. Cut an arrow out of colored paper and attach it to the center of the plate with a paper fastener.

A SHOFAR TO SEW

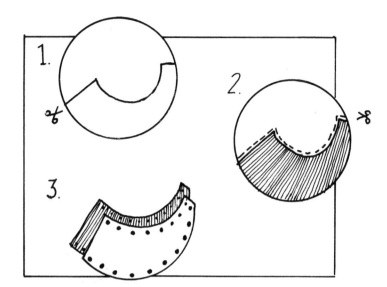

What You Need:

Two paper plates
Hole punch
Yarn, string, or shoelaces
Scissors

What You Do:

1. Cut out a shofar shape from a paper plate.

2. Turn the shape over and trace it on another paper plate. Cut it out.

3. Place the two shapes together to form a shofar. Punch holes along the two sides and sew together with yarn, string, or shoelaces. Don't forget to tie a knot at each end.

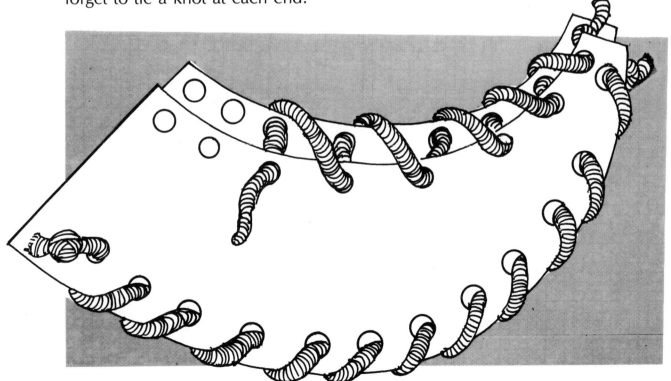

NEW YEAR CARDS

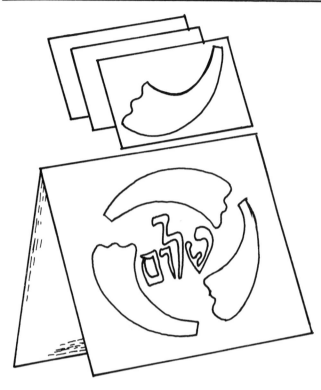

HOLIDAY SHAPES

What You Need:

Colored paper
Crayons or markers
Scissors and glue

What You Do:

1. Put three small sheets of different colored paper together. Draw a holiday design on the top sheet. Cut out the design with all three papers together.

2. Fold a larger piece of colored paper in half. Glue the three shapes in a pretty design on the outside. Write a special New Year message and sign your name inside.

CUT-OUTS

What You Need:

2 colors of construction paper
Glue, pencil, scissors

What You Do:

1. Fold one piece of paper in half to form a card. Cut the other piece of paper half as wide as the front of the card. Draw the shape of half of a wine cup along one edge. Cut it out. Save both pieces.

2. Glue the cut piece of paper to the front of the card. Make it even with the top and bottom and folded side of the card.

3. Turn the cut-out shape over and glue it to the other half of the wine cup. Write your holiday message inside.

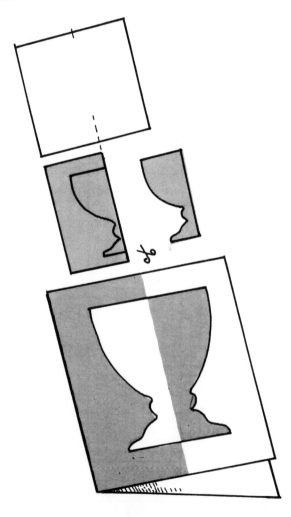

20

MOSAIC CARD

What You Need:

Colored tissue paper
Colored construction paper
Glue, scissors

What You Do:

1. Cut a rectangle from construction paper and fold into thirds. Unfold. Fold the bottom third back underneath the middle section.

2. Draw a shofar, an apple, or another Rosh Hashanah symbol in the center of the middle section. Do not let it reach the edges. Punch a hole in the center of your drawing, and cut out the shape from the bottom and middle sections at the same time.

3. Turn the card over and unfold. Paste strips of colored tissue paper to cover all the cut-out space in the middle section. Put glue on the edges of the bottom section and fold it up over the middle section.

4. Now write a New Year message on the card.

FAMILY NEW YEAR CARDS

PHOTO CARD

What You Need:

Photo of your family
Construction paper
Scissors, glue, markers

What You Do:

1. Ask permission to use a recent photo of your family.

2. Fold a piece of construction paper in half to make a card. Paste the photo on the front.

3. Draw a frame around the photo and decorate. Or, you can cut a frame out of another piece of paper and paste it over your photo.

4. Write SHANAH TOVAH (Happy New Year) inside and sign your name. Photo cards are especially nice for relatives who live far away.

HANDPRINT CARD

What You Need:

Construction paper
Crayons or markers

What You Do:

1. Fold a piece of construction paper in half to make a card.

2. Have family members trace their hands and write their names inside.

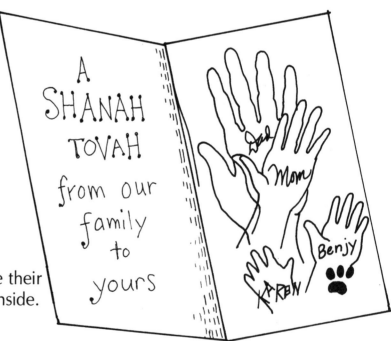

You can send your handprint card along with your photo card for a double New Year greeting!

SHANAH TOVAH MAILBAG

What You Need:

Large paper bag
Yarn
Crayons, markers, scissors, glue, stapler

What You Do:

1. Cut a large rectangle from the paper bag. Fold in half and unfold. On the bottom half, cut off a narrow strip on each side.

2. Fold the rectangle in half again, and fold the ends over the middle section. Glue closed.

3. Cut a piece of yarn big enough to go over your shoulder. Staple to the bag to form a handle.

4. Decorate the mailbag with Rosh Hashanah symbols.

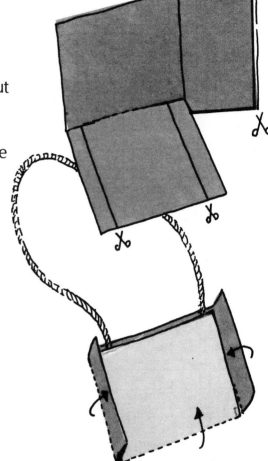

A STRING OF NEW YEAR CARDS

What You Need:

New Year cards
Hole punch
Long string or yarn

What You Do:

1. Did the mailman bring lots of pretty New Year cards to your house? Ask a grown-up if you can use them.

2. Punch a hole in the top two corners of each card. Weave a long string in and out through the holes. Leave extra string at each end so you can tie your cards to a window or door.

ROUND CHALLAH COVER

What You Need:

Large round paper doily
Colored paper
Scissors, glue, crayons, or markers

What You Do:

1. Cut a circle the same size as the doily out of colored paper. Glue the doily onto the circle.

2. Cut out Rosh Hashanah designs from different colored paper and glue them on the doily.

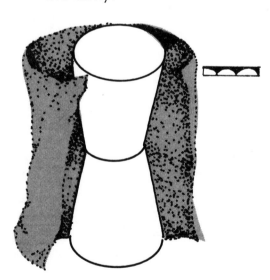

A SILVER KIDDUSH CUP

What You Need:

Three paper or plastic cups, all the same size
Aluminum foil
Decorating scraps (colored paper, felt, macaroni)
Glue or tape

What You Do:

1. Glue or tape the bottoms of the two cups together. Cover them with aluminum foil. Make designs out of the scraps and glue them on.

2. Put the third cup inside to hold the wine.

CANDLESTICKS FOR YOM TOV

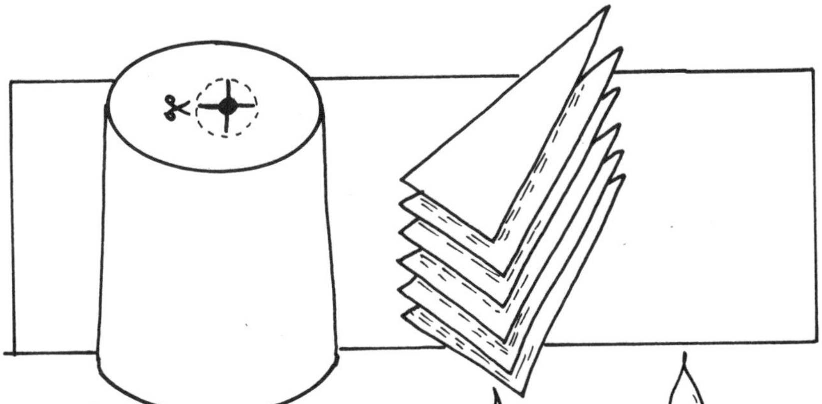

What You Need:

Styrofoam cup
Cardboard
Aluminum foil
Scissors, glue
Candles

What You Do:

1. Make a small hole in the bottom of the cup. A candle should fit snugly into it. Try it to make sure. Cover the outside of the cup with foil. Push the foil in where the hole is.

2. Cut out six long cardboard triangles all the same size. Cover them with foil. Glue them onto the cup around the hole to form a star. Let it dry overnight.

3. Cover the bottom of a candle with foil and place it into the hole.

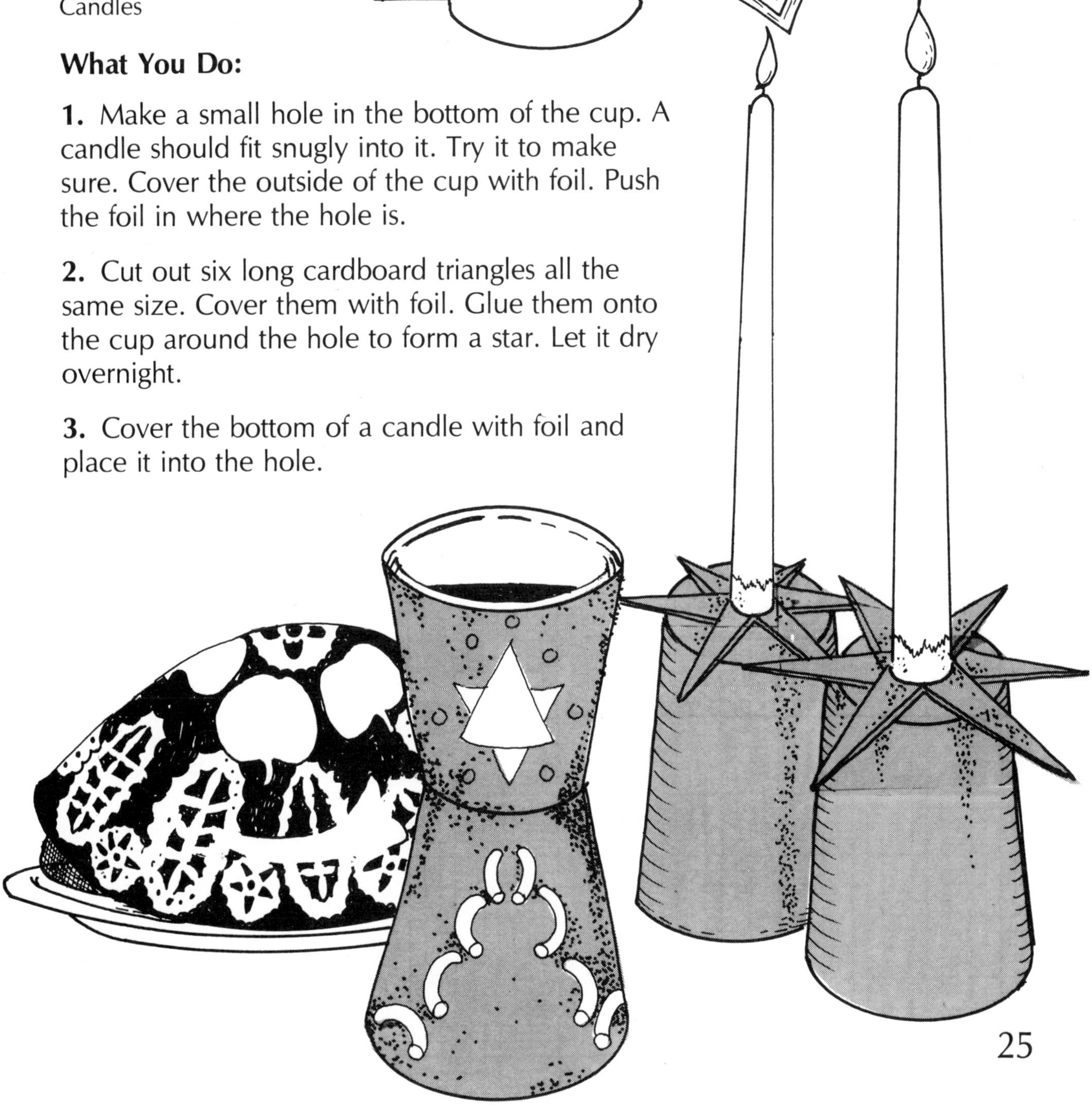

APPLE AND HONEY DISH

What You Need:

Large paper plate
Small paper plate
Muffin cup
Crayons, paints, decorating scraps
Scissors, glue
Apples and honey

What You Do:

1. Make pretty designs around the edge of the larger plate. Glue the small paper plate onto the larger plate.

2. Glue a muffin cup in the center of the smaller plate. Pour honey into it. Put apple slices around it and enjoy a sweet holiday treat.

SOMETHING SWEET TO EAT

What You Need:

10 tsp powdered sugar
1 tsp water
2 drops food coloring
Toothpicks
Graham crackers

What You Do:

1. Make icing by mixing together powdered sugar, water, and food coloring.

2. Use a toothpick as your "brush" and icing as your "paint" to draw holiday designs on graham crackers.

26

TABLE CENTERPIECE

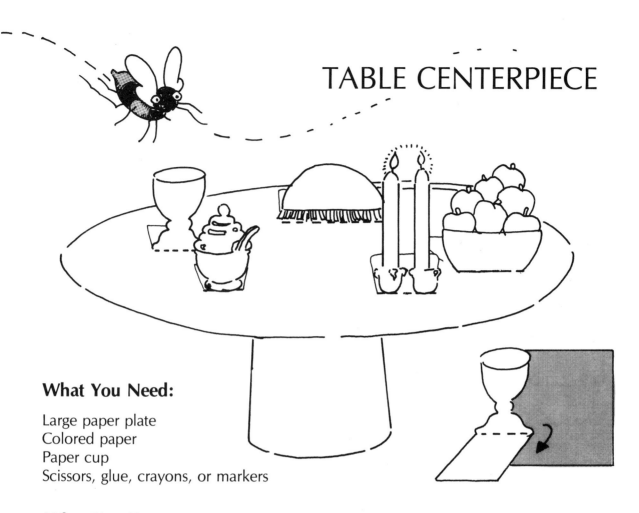

What You Need:

Large paper plate
Colored paper
Paper cup
Scissors, glue, crayons, or markers

What You Do:

1. Draw pictures of a round challah, kiddush cup, candlesticks, dish of honey, and bowl of apples. Cut them out, leaving a tab at the bottom. You may trace the shapes below.

2. Put glue on the picture tabs and attach to paper plate. Glue the plate onto an inverted paper cup.

SUKKOT

Sukkot is a fall harvest holiday. We build temporary booths (sukkot) and decorate them with branches and fruit to celebrate the crops that provide our food. We eat, study, play, and sometimes sleep in our sukkah during the holiday. We remember that when the Jewish people wandered in the desert after they were freed from slavery in Egypt, they built sukkot for shade and rest.

WORDS TO KNOW

Sukkot — the harvest holiday of booths

Sukkah — harvest booth (plural: Sukkot)

S'chach — leafy roof of the sukkah

Lulav — palm branch bound with willow and myrtle branches which symbolizes the harvest

Etrog — lemon-like citron

Ushpizin — guests from history we invite to the sukkah

SUKKOT

LULAV AND ETROG

What You Need:

Long cardboard roll
Two egg carton cups
Green construction paper
Green and yellow tissue paper
Glue, tape, scissors
Brown marker

What You Do:

To Make Etrog:

1. Cut two cups from the egg carton and glue together.

2. Spread glue all over and cover with yellow tissue. Etrogs are bumpy!

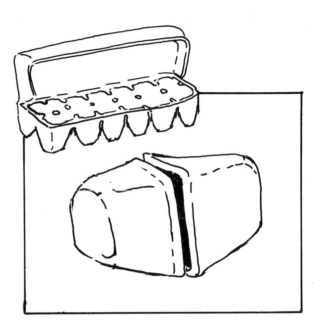

SUKKAH GUESTS (USHPIZIN)

What You Need:

Paper
Cotton, fabric, yarn, crayons
Scissors, glue

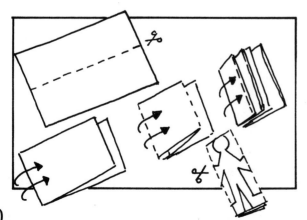

What You Do:

1. Cut a piece of paper in half lengthwise. Discard one piece.

2. Fold the other piece in half three times, so you have eight panels. Cut off and discard one of the end panels. Draw a figure and cut out as shown, making sure not to cut at the hands and feet. Unfold carefully.

3. Decorate your seven ushpizin (visitors) to look like our ancestors.

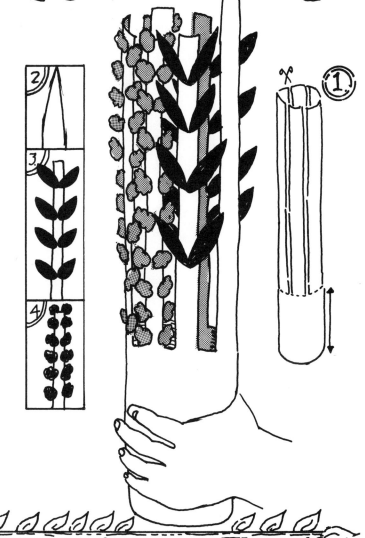

To Make Lulav:

1. Cut the cardboard roll into six strips, stopping about three inches from the bottom.

2. *For the palm branch:* Cut the corners off one strip to make it pointy. Color it brown.

3. *For the two willow branches:* Cut about an inch off the top of two strips. Cut leaves out of green construction paper and paste onto the two strips.

4. *For the three myrtle branches:* Cut about an inch off the three remaining strips. Crumple small bits of green tissue and glue them onto the three strips.

To Use:

Hold the etrog in your left hand and the lulav in your right. Shake them together up, down, and all around you.

ABRAHAM   ISAAC   JACOB   JOSEPH   MOSES   AARON   DAVID

A FRIENDLY BEE

What You Do:

1. Wrap yellow tissue paper around the cardboard roll and tuck in the ends. Draw black bee stripes around the roll.

2. Make a yellow tissue ball for the head and push it into one end of the roll. Glue two beans for eyes and black yarn for feelers.

3. Cut wings from white tissue paper and glue or tape them on. Tape six short pieces of black yarn for legs.

4. Fasten a long piece of yarn to the bee's body and hang it in the sukkah.

What You Need:

Small cardboard roll
White and yellow tissue paper
Black yarn
Two black beans
Black marker
Scissors, glue, tape

BUTTERFLY

What You Need:

Scrap material
String
Felt
Pipe cleaner
Spring clothespin
Glue, scissors

What You Do:

1. Cut an oval about 3″ × 4″ from colorful scrap material.

2. Gather it at the center with a piece of string and glue it to a spring clothespin.

3. Glue a strip of felt on top for the body. Add eyes and pieces of pipe cleaner for antennae.

4. Clip your butterfly to the branches of your sukkah.

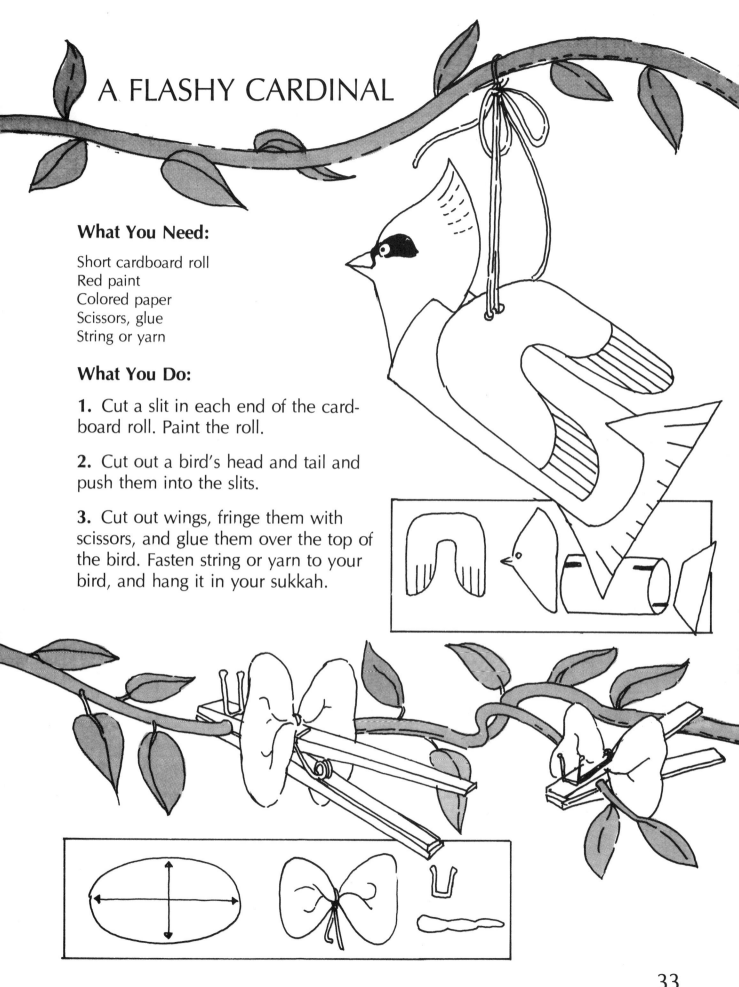

A FLASHY CARDINAL

What You Need:

Short cardboard roll
Red paint
Colored paper
Scissors, glue
String or yarn

What You Do:

1. Cut a slit in each end of the cardboard roll. Paint the roll.

2. Cut out a bird's head and tail and push them into the slits.

3. Cut out wings, fringe them with scissors, and glue them over the top of the bird. Fasten string or yarn to your bird, and hang it in your sukkah.

33

A BOUNCY SPIDER ON A WEB

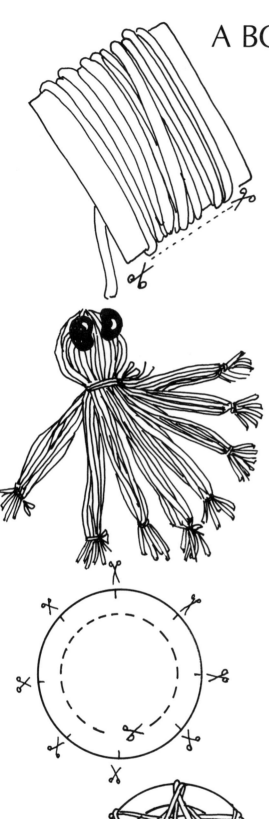

What You Need:

White and black yarn
Sturdy paper or plastic plate
Cardboard (½ piece of shirt cardboard works well)
Two colored beans
Scissors

What You Do:

For spider:

1. Wrap black yarn around and around the cardboard. The length of the cardboard will be size of your spider.

2. Cut all the strands at the bottom and carefully remove cardboard. Tie a piece of yarn at the neck, and plump out the yarn for the head.

3. Separate the loose yarn into eight equal groups and tie a piece of yarn at the end of each to form eight legs.

For web:

1. Cut the center out of a paper plate, keeping the rim intact. Cut small notches around the outside of the rim.

2. Wrap a long strand of white yarn back and forth around the plate, through the notches. Keep a few inches of yarn at the end to hang your web.

3. Tie each leg of the spider to a strand of web, and hang on a branch in your sukkah.

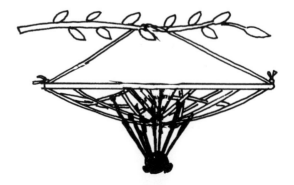

34

WIND CHIMES

What You Need:

2 popsicle sticks
Yarn
16 frozen juice caps
Glue

What You Do:

1. Glue popsicle sticks to form an X, and bind together with yarn.

2. Cut four, foot-long pieces of yarn, and glue three juice caps evenly spaced along each piece, leaving 3" at one end.

3. Cut one, 18-inch piece of yarn, and glue on four caps.

4. Tie the strands to the X, with the long piece in the center, leaving a piece to attach your wind chimes to your sukkah roof.

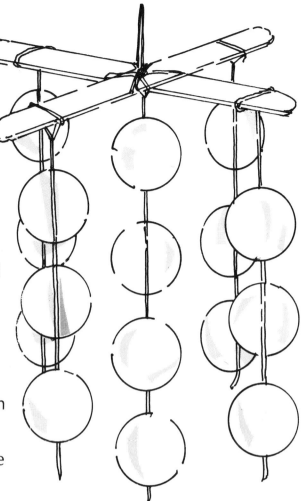

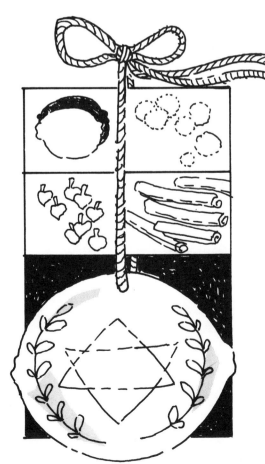

SPICE HANGERS

What You Need:

Felt, trimming scraps, glitter
Cotton balls
Spices (cloves, cinnamon stick pieces)
Glue, scissors

What You Do:

1. Cut out two, identical fruit shapes from felt.

2. Glue them together at the edges, leaving an opening at the top.

3. Decorate both sides with trimming scraps and/or glitter.

4. Fill with cotton balls and spices and glue closed.

5. Add yarn or rick-rack edging, and a loop for hanging.

35

FRUIT MOSAIC

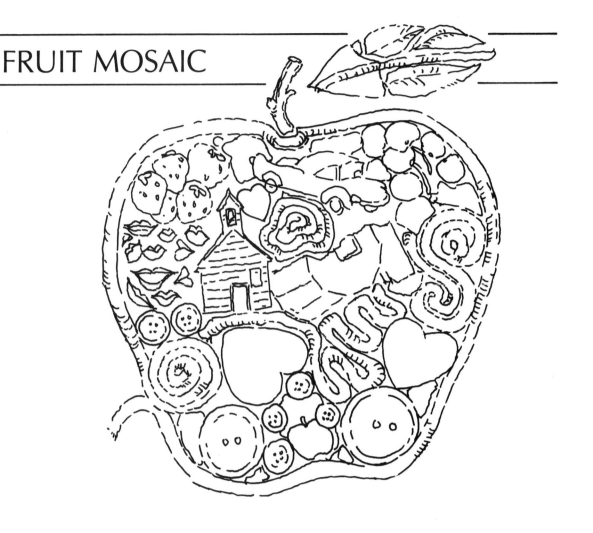

What You Need:

Large piece of card-
board or poster
board
Decorating scraps
(cut-up magazine
pictures, string, yarn,
cloth, tissue paper,
leaves, buttons, etc.)
Glue, scissors

What You Do:

1. Draw a fruit shape on heavy paper and cut it
out.

2. Paste different kinds of scraps all over your
fruit shape. Try to use scraps the same color as
your fruit, but vary the shades and textures.

3. Make several fruit mosaics to hang in your
sukkah.

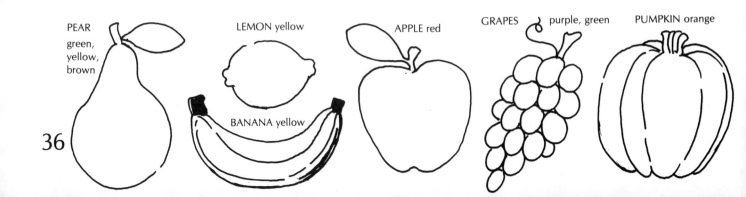

PEAR green, yellow, brown

LEMON yellow

BANANA yellow

APPLE red

GRAPES purple, green

PUMPKIN orange

BEAN MOSAIC

What You Need:

Seeds and beans
Paper plate
Glue
Pencil
Ribbon or string

What You Do:

1. Draw a holiday design on a paper plate.

2. Spread glue on one section at a time, and fill in with beans or seeds. Shake off the extras. Continue until your design is filled.

3. Punch two holes and string ribbon through the top of the plate. Your bean mosaic is ready to hang.

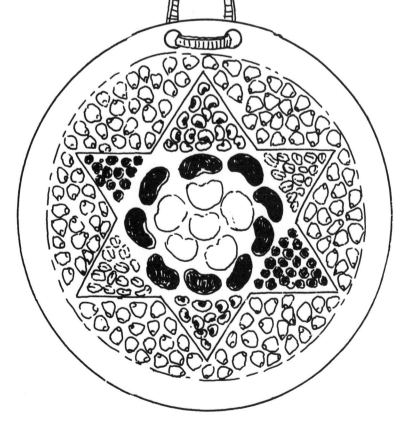

TABLE-TOP SUKKAH

What You Need:

Tissue or shoe box
Drinking straws
Hole punch
Old magazines
Colored paper or paint
Leaves or greens
Scissors, glue

What You Do:

1. Cut the top off a tissue box, or use a shoe box without the lid. Cut out a door. Paint the sides, or cover them with colored paper. If you use paint, mix it with liquid detergent to help it stick better. Cut out pictures of colorful fruits and vegetables from old magazines. Use them to decorate the inside walls.

2. Punch holes across the tops on the two long sides. Push straws through the holes. Put pretty leaves or greens on top of the straws.

3. Invite your play people to a sukkah party.

A FRUIT SNACK

What You Need:

Apples, pears, bananas
Peanut butter, honey, or jam
Wheat germ
Bowl, knife

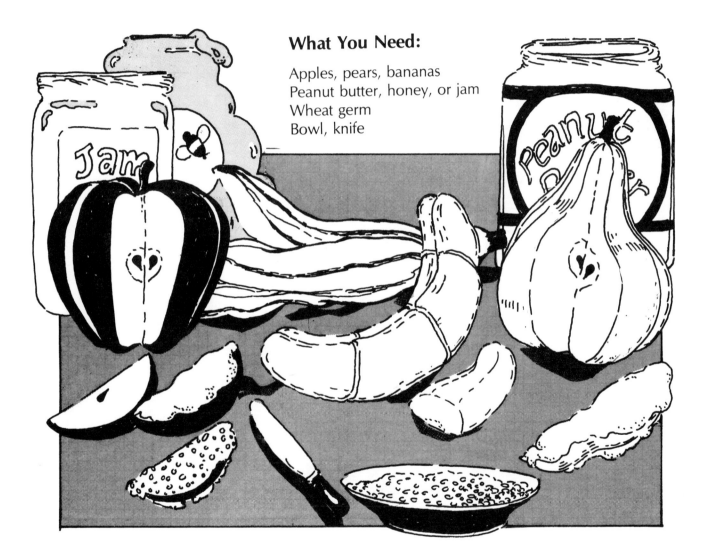

What You Do:

1. Slice the fruit into wedges.

2. Spread peanut butter, honey, or jam on both sides of the wedges.
Dip into a dish of wheat germ.

3. Enjoy your fruit snacks in your sukkah.

SIMCHAT TORAH ———————————

Each year in synagogue, we read the Torah from start to finish. The holiday of Simchat Torah marks the day we finish reading the last section and begin reading the first section over again. Dance, sing, and wave your flag! It's time for a Torah parade.

WORDS TO KNOW

Simchat Torah — Rejoicing in the Torah

Torah — first five books of the Bible, written on a parchment scroll, and read in synagogue

Keter — silver crown on the Torah

Yad — pointer used to read the Torah

Aliyah — honor of being called to recite the Torah blessings

Kippah — headcovering; yarmulke

SIMCHAT TORAH

TORAH MOBILE

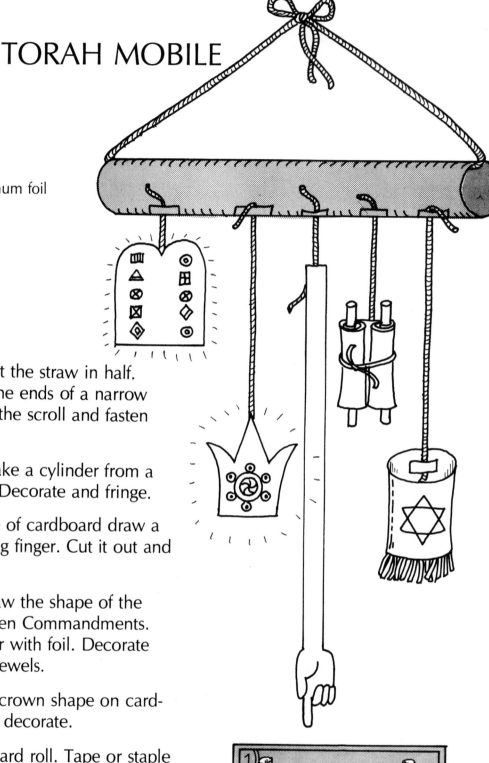

What You Need:

Large cardboard roll
Colored paper, aluminum foil
Cardboard
Yarn, colorful fabric
Drinking straw
Tape, stapler, scissors
Wire twister
Paint and paintbrush

What You Do:

1. Torah Scroll: Cut the straw in half. Tape each half to the ends of a narrow strip of paper. Roll the scroll and fasten with a wire twister.

2. Torah cover: Make a cylinder from a rectangle of fabric. Decorate and fringe.

3. Yad: On a piece of cardboard draw a hand with a pointing finger. Cut it out and decorate.

4. Breast plate: Draw the shape of the two tablets of the Ten Commandments. Cut it out and cover with foil. Decorate with make-believe jewels.

5. Crown: Draw a crown shape on cardboard, cut out, and decorate.

6. Paint the cardboard roll. Tape or staple a piece of yarn to each object and tape the other ends to the cardboard roll. Make each piece of yarn a different length.

7. Push a long piece of yarn through the roll and tie the ends together.

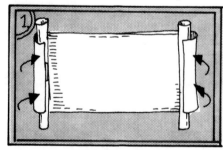

PAPER TORAH

What You Need:

Plastic or paper straws
White paper (legal size)
Crayons, markers, scissors, tape
Colored paper
Ribbon or yarn

What You Do:

1. Cut a long strip of paper 4"
high. Tape each end to the middle
of a straw, and roll up.

2. Tie with ribbon or yarn.

3. Cut a strip of colored paper big
enough to fit around the Torah.
Draw designs and fringe bottom.

4. Place the strip around the Torah
and tape the edges together.

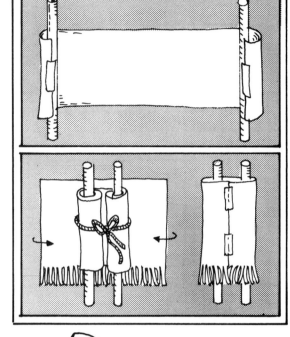

ISRAEL'S FLAG

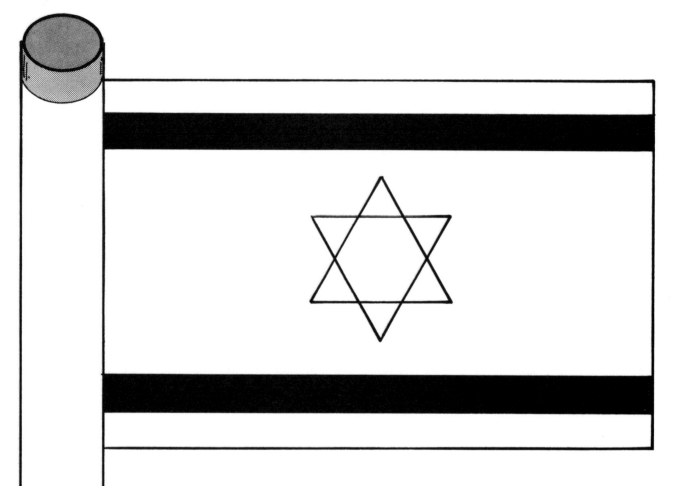

What You Need:

Long cardboard roll
White paper
Blue crayon or paint
Scissors, glue

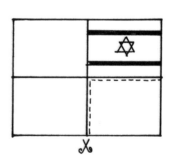 

What You Do:

1. Fold the paper into four parts. Cut out one part as shown in the picture.

2. Decorate the flag with a blue stripe near the top, a blue stripe near the bottom, and a blue star in the center.

3. Glue the other sections around the cardboard roll.

COLORFUL KIPPAH

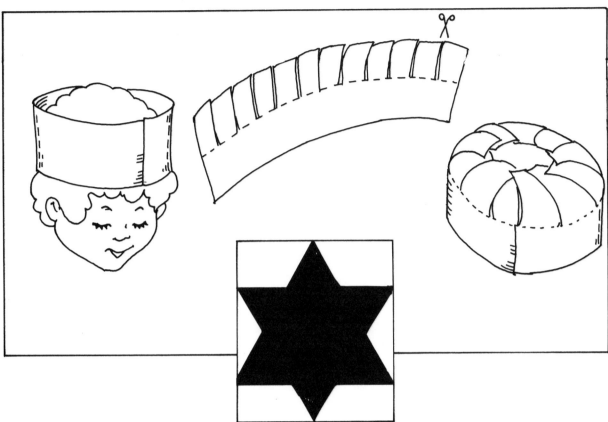

What You Need:

Colored paper
Glue, scissors

What You Do:

1. Make a wide headband from a long piece of colored paper. Tape it together to fit your head.

2. Cut evenly-spaced slits around the top of the headband. Glue each tab over the one next to it.

3. Cut out a Jewish star from a different colored paper. Glue it down to cover the top of the crown.

45

HANUKKAH

Hanukkah celebrates the victory of the Maccabees, a small band of Jewish patriots, over the mighty armies of Syrian King Antiochus. When they restored the Holy Temple in Jerusalem, the Maccabees found one jar of pure oil, enough to keep the menorah burning for just one day. But a miracle happened, and the oil burned for eight days. Each night of the holiday, we light one more candle, exchange gifts, play dreidel, and eat fried latkes and donuts to remember this victory for religious freedom and the miracle of the oil.

WORDS TO KNOW

Hanukkah — Festival of Lights — the word means "dedication"

Menorah — eight-branch candle holder (the Hebrew word is "hanukkiah")

Shamash — helper candle used to light the other candles

Dreidel — spinning top with four Hebrew letters (nun, gimmel, hey, shin) which stand for "Nes Gadol Hayah Sham," "A Great Miracle Happened There". The Hebrew word for dreidel is "sevivon."

Latkes — pancakes

Judah Maccabee — hero of the Hanukkah story

HANUKKAH

AN OIL MENORAH

What You Need:

9 metal bottle caps
1 long and 1 short block of wood
   (ask a lumber yard for scraps)
Pipe cleaners
9 small nails
Small jar of olive oil

What You Do:

1. Nail the eight bottle caps in a row on the long block of wood, leaving a space at one end.

2. Nail the ninth bottle cap to the small block, and glue the block onto the space at the end of the larger block, for the shamash.

3. Cut pipe cleaners into one-inch pieces to form wicks.

4. Pour a small bit of oil into each bottle cap and place the end of one wick in each. Make sure a grown-up helps you light your oil menorah.

What You Need:

Strips of colored paper
Scissors
Glue or stapler
Masking tape or pins

What You Do:

1. Staple or glue one strip together to form a ring. Put another strip through the ring and fasten it to make another ring. Make a large chain of rings for the outer part of your menorah. Make smaller chains for each branch.

2. Use masking tape to attach your menorah to a window or a wall, or pin it to a curtain.

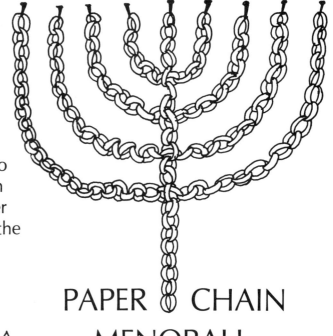

PAPER ⊗ CHAIN MENORAH

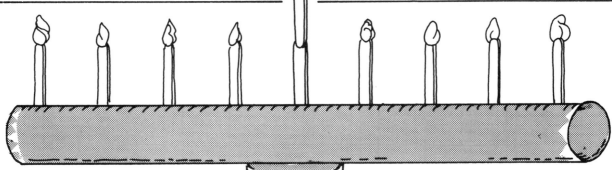

What You Need:

Large cardboard roll
Paper cup with flat bottom
Ten popsicle sticks
Yellow tissue paper
Paints, glue, scissors

A MENORAH YOU CAN "LIGHT"

What You Do:

1. With the scissors, make nine slits across the top of a cardboard tube. Glue the tube to the paper cup. Decorate.

2. Paint the popsicle sticks. Glue two of them together to make the tall shamash. Paste yellow tissue paper to the top of each stick for flames.

3. Place your shamash in the menorah and add one candle each night of Hanukkah.

49

What You Need:

Colored paper
Yellow or orange tissue paper
Crayons or markers, glue

What You Do:

1. Place your left hand on the left side of a sheet of paper so your wrist is even with the bottom. Spread your fingers. Start at the bottom and trace around your four fingers. Don't trace your thumb!

2. Put your right hand on the right side of the paper and trace around your four right fingers.

3. Draw a large "candle" in the middle and connect it to your "candle" fingers.

4. Color the Hanukkiah and each of the candles. Glue bits of tissue paper for the flames.

HANUKKAH HOT PLATE

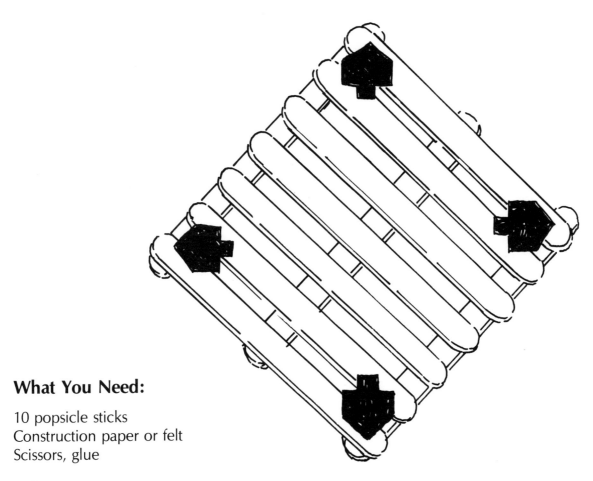

What You Need:

10 popsicle sticks
Construction paper or felt
Scissors, glue

What You Do:

1. Put glue across three popsicle sticks. Space the dry sticks across the three glued ones. Make the ends and edges touch.

2. Cut out Hanukkah shapes from construction paper or felt and paste them on the hotplate.

RECYCLED DREIDEL

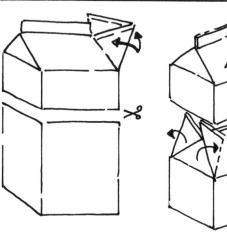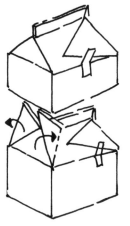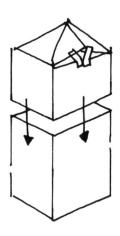

What You Need:

Clean, dry milk carton
Pictures from old magazines or junk mail
Dried-out thick marker
Scissors, glue, strong tape, marker

What You Do:

1. Cut the milk carton about three inches from the spout. Bend the open spouts backwards, flat against the carton, and tape down.

2. Open the other side of the spout and tape those pieces down as well. This will leave a point in the middle.

3. Slide the spout end of the carton over the bottom half.

4. Glue a collage of pictures on the dreidel, and write the Hebrew letters nun, gimmel, hey, and shin on each side.

5. Make a hole in the bottom and poke a marker through for a handle. Spin the dreidel and see which letter lands on top.

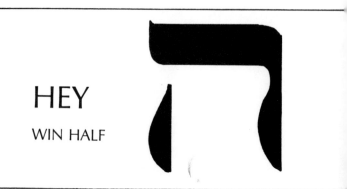

GIMMEL

WIN ALL

HEY

WIN HALF

DREIDEL SPINNER

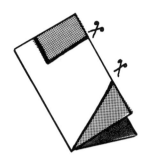

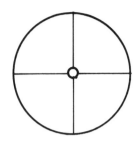

What You Do:

1. Fold paper in half. Draw half a dreidel along the fold, and cut out.

2. Draw lines across and down the middle of the paper plate to divide it into quarters. Write the dreidel rules around the rim of the plate.

3. Fasten the dreidel shape to the center of the plate. Make the hole big enough so your dreidel spins easily.

What You Need:

Paper plate
Colored paper
Markers
Paper fastener

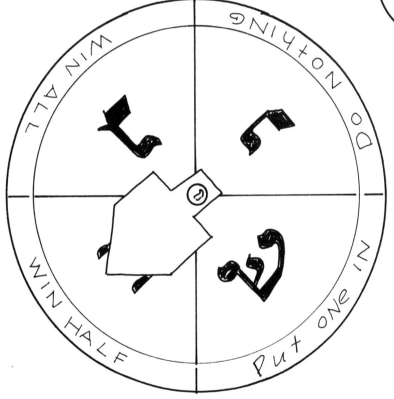

If the dreidel point lands on a line, spin again!

NUN

DO NOTHING

SHIN

PUT ONE IN

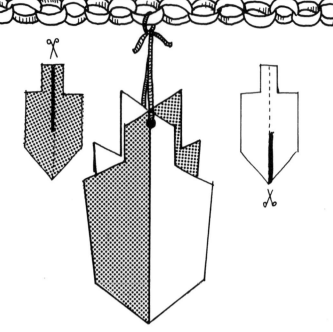

HANUKKAH CHAIN

What You Need:

Strips of colored paper
Scissors, glue, stapler
String

What You Do:

1. Staple or glue one strip together to form a ring. Put another strip through the ring and fasten it to make a second ring. Continue until the chain is as long as you want it.

2. Make dreidel decorations and hang them from the chain.

SPINNING DREIDEL

What You Need:

Construction paper
Markers, scissors, hole punch
String or yarn

What You Do:

1. Put two pieces of paper together and fold them in half. Draw half a dreidel shape along the fold.

2. Cut out. Slit the dreidels along the fold, one from the top to the center, and the other from the bottom to the center.

3. Slide the two together through the slits.

4. Punch a small hole in the top of one of the dreidels and hang with string or yarn.

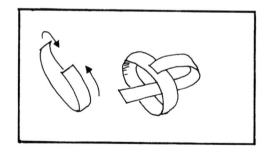

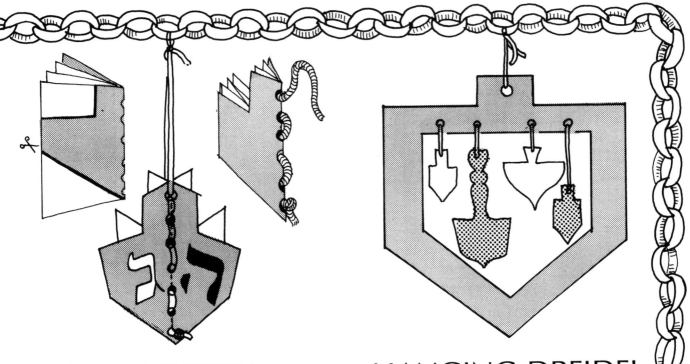

SEWN DREIDEL

What You Need:

Colored paper
Hole punch, scissors
Yarn

What You Do:

1. Put two pieces of paper together and fold them in half. Draw half a dreidel shape along the fold and cut out.

2. Punch holes along the fold and then unfold the dreidels.

3. Knot one end of the yarn. Beginning at the bottom, sew in and out of the holes until you reach the top. Leave extra yarn to hang your dreidel.

An idea! Use your leftover paper to copy or trace the Hebrew letters on pages 52-53. Cut out and paste on your dreidel.

HANGING DREIDEL

What You Need:

White shirt cardboard
Colored paper
Thread or thin yarn
Scissors, glue, markers

What You Do:

1. Draw and cut out a large dreidel shape from the cardboard. Draw a smaller dreidel shape inside the big one, and cut out the inside dreidel.

2. Cut four small dreidel shapes from different colored paper. Cut four pieces of yarn or thread. Glue one end to each small dreidel and the other to the big dreidel frame.

3. Glue a long piece of yarn to the handle of the large dreidel and hang.

PAPER BAG PUPPET

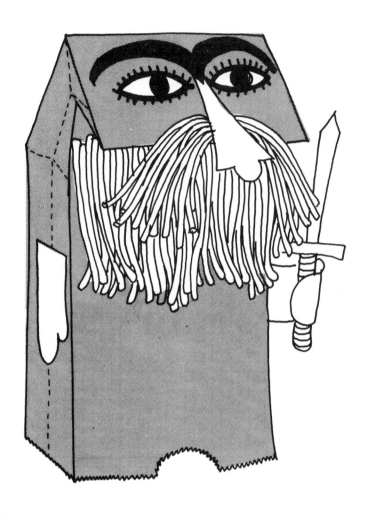

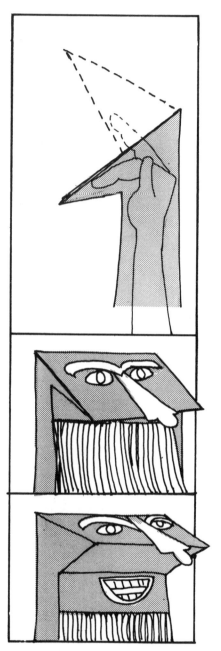

What You Need:

Small paper bag (brown lunch bag works best)
Colored paper or decorating scraps
Scissors, glue

What You Do:

1. On the flap of the paper bag, glue colored shapes to look like hair, eyes, and nose. Glue a small strip of red paper under the flap for the mouth.

2. Cut out arms and paste them on the sides of the bag. For Judah Maccabee, glue a sword in one hand and a shield in the other.

Make puppets for all the Hanukkah characters and put on a show!

SHOE PUPPET

What You Need:

A shoe
Construction paper
Decorating scraps
Popsicle stick
Scissors, markers, glue

What You Do:

1. Draw around your shoe and cut out.

2. Cut paper arms and legs from construction paper and glue to the back of your shoe body. Glue popsicle stick to back.

3. Draw a face on the front of your shoe puppet, and add clothing, hair, and other decorations.

PAPER PLATE PUPPET

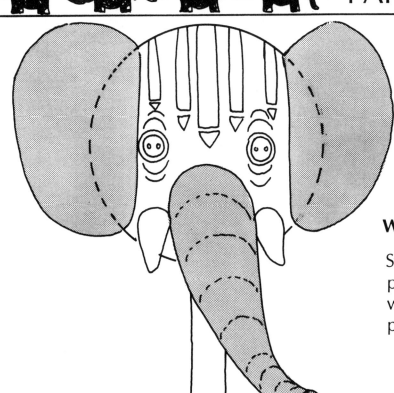

What You Need:

Small paper plate
Popsicle stick
Decorating scraps
Scissors, glue, stapler

What You Do:

Staple a popsicle stick to a paper plate. Decorate your puppet face with yarn, buttons, cotton, colored paper, foil, or crayons.

A COUPON GIFT

What You Need:

Construction paper
Scissors, stapler, markers, or crayons

What You Do:

1. Fold two pieces of construction paper in thirds and cut out. This is enough for five coupons and a cover.

2. Write or draw a promise on each coupon. Decorate the cover for dad or mom.

A LAPBOARD

What You Need:

Cardboard
Self-stick shelf paper
Envelope, small pad
Pen, markers, scissors, glue, string

What You Do:

1. Cover cardboard with pretty, self-stick paper. Write or paste the name on top.

2. Cut the flap off an envelope and discard. Paste the envelope to the board. Put a pad inside it.

3. Poke a hole in the corner and tie a thin marker to the lapboard.

PERSONALIZED BOOKMARK

What You Need:

Window envelope (a used one is ok)
Alphabet noodles - Hebrew or English
Colored paper
Scissors, glue

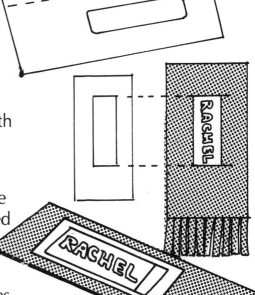

What You Do:

1. Cut a long rectangle from the envelope with the window in the middle.

2. Cut a piece of colored paper a little larger than the window. Find the letters for the name you wish to make. Glue them onto the colored paper.

3. Put glue around the edges of the window and fasten it to the colored paper. Fringe edges.

HANUKKAH WRAPPING PAPER

What You Need:

Food coloring (or paint)
Paper towels
Small bowl
Hanukkah cookie cutters or other shapes
Plain white shelf paper

What You Do:

1. Mix a few drops of food coloring with a few spoonfuls of water to make a color you like.

2. Fold two paper towels to fit in a small flat bowl. Pour just enough colored water on the paper towels to make a moist pad.

3. Press a Hanukkah cookie cutter on the pad and then on the paper. Add more colored water if your pad gets too dry. Make a pretty design all over your wrapping paper.

DREIDEL THANK-YOU NOTES

What You Need:

White paper
Scissors
Crayons or markers
Envelopes

What You Do:

1. Draw or trace a dreidel and cut out.

2. Fold each side to the middle and write "Thank You" on the flaps. Decorate.

3. Write or draw your "thank-you" message inside, and sign your name.

4. Put in envelope to mail or deliver.

HANUKKAH GAMES

SUFGANIYOT SCRAMBLE

Tie a 12-inch string around each sufganiyah (donut). Each player must put the end of the string into his or her mouth, and at the signal, chew up the string. The first person to take a bite is the winner. Hands behind your back, please!

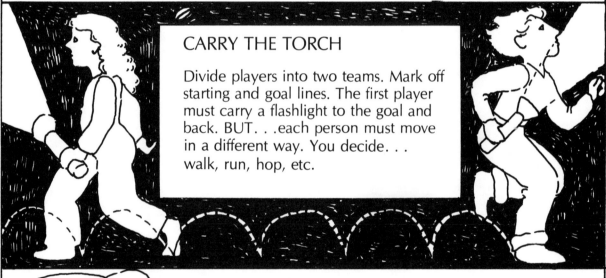

CARRY THE TORCH

Divide players into two teams. Mark off starting and goal lines. The first player must carry a flashlight to the goal and back. BUT. . .each person must move in a different way. You decide. . . walk, run, hop, etc.

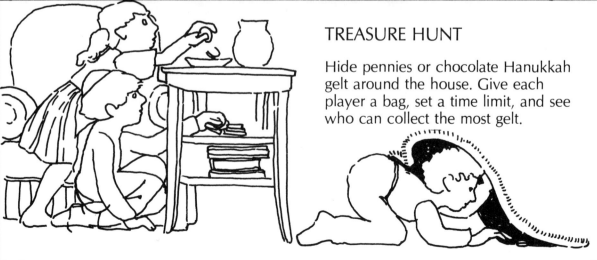

TREASURE HUNT

Hide pennies or chocolate Hanukkah gelt around the house. Give each player a bag, set a time limit, and see who can collect the most gelt.

LIGHT THE MENORAH

Make a playing board like the one in the diagram, and cut out a small candle playing piece for each guest. (Number them or make them different colors so players will know their own pieces.) Each time a player answers a question correctly, (s)he moves one space ahead. The first to place a candle in the menorah is the winner. Here are some questions you may ask. Try to think up others.

Round 1: Potato latkes are a favorite Hanukkah treat. Everyone name something else made from potatoes.

Round 2: We light candles on Hanukkah. Everyone name another time when we light candles.

Round 3: Judah Maccabee was a Jewish hero. Everyone name another Jewish hero.

Round 4: There are four Hebrew letters on the dreidel, but 22 in the Hebrew alphabet. Everyone name a Hebrew letter.

Round 5: The Maccabees rebuilt the Temple. Everyone name something you find in a Temple or Synagogue today.

Round 6: Hanukkah is a time for gift-giving. Everyone name another time we give gifts.

Round 7: A dreidel spins. Everyone name something else that spins.

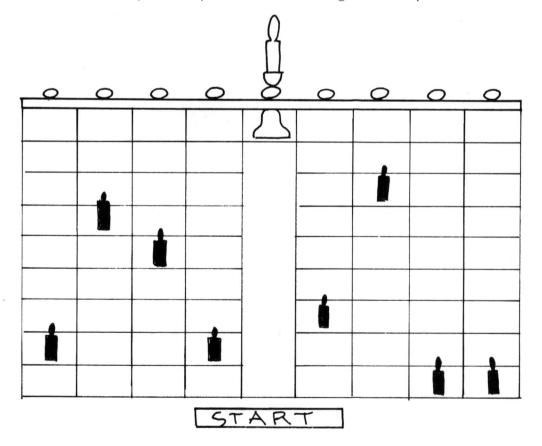

START

DREIDEL SANDWICHES

What You Need:

Bread and filling
Carrot or celery stick
Cheese, pickle, or peppers

Make your favorite sandwich and trim crusts. Slice diagonally and then in half. Top with carrot or celery stick handle and make dreidel letter with cheese, pickle, or pepper strips.

CANDY DREIDELS

What You Need:

Candy kiss or marshmallow
Toothpick

Push a toothpick into a candy kiss or marshmallow for a sweet dreidel treat.

CANDLE SALAD

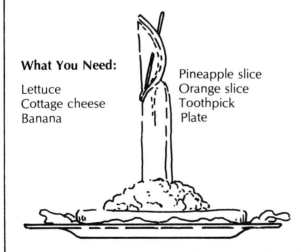

What You Need:

Lettuce
Cottage cheese
Banana

Pineapple slice
Orange slice
Toothpick
Plate

Put a pineapple slice on a lettuce leaf and top with a mound of cottage cheese. Cut a banana in half and put one part in the center. Fasten a small slice of orange to the top of the banana with a toothpick to make the flame.

EDIBLE MENORAH

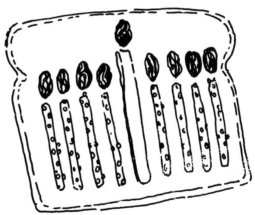

What You Need:

Bread
Raisins

Carrot stick
Eight pretzel sticks
Cream cheese or butter
Plastic knife

Spread soft butter or cream cheese on a piece of bread and top with pretzel stick candles and a carrot stick shamash. Use raisins for flames.

TU B'SHEVAT

Tu B'Shevat is the birthday of the trees. In Israel the almond tree begins to bloom, telling us spring is here. It is a time to plant trees and flowers and to think about protecting and preserving our good earth. Celebrate with a snack of tasty fruits and nuts.

WORDS TO KNOW

Tu B'Shevat — the 15th of Shevat, birthday of the trees

JNF — Jewish National Fund — Israel's agency responsible for planting trees and reclaiming the land

Tzedakah Box — container for collecting coins for charity

TU B'SHEVAT

RECYCLER

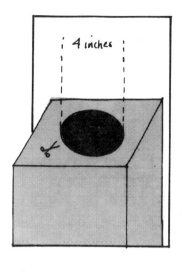

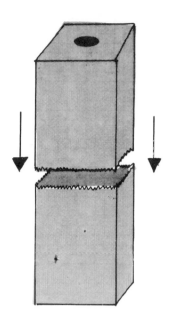

What You Need:

2 large grocery bags
Markers or crayons
Scissors

What You Do:

1. Cut a 4″ hole in the bottom of a large grocery bag.

2. Turn over and decorate the sides to look like a tree, a monster, a robot, or whatever you like.

3. Fit the bag over another paper bag. Drop your cans and jars into the recycler. When the bag is full, place the recycler over another empty bag.

66

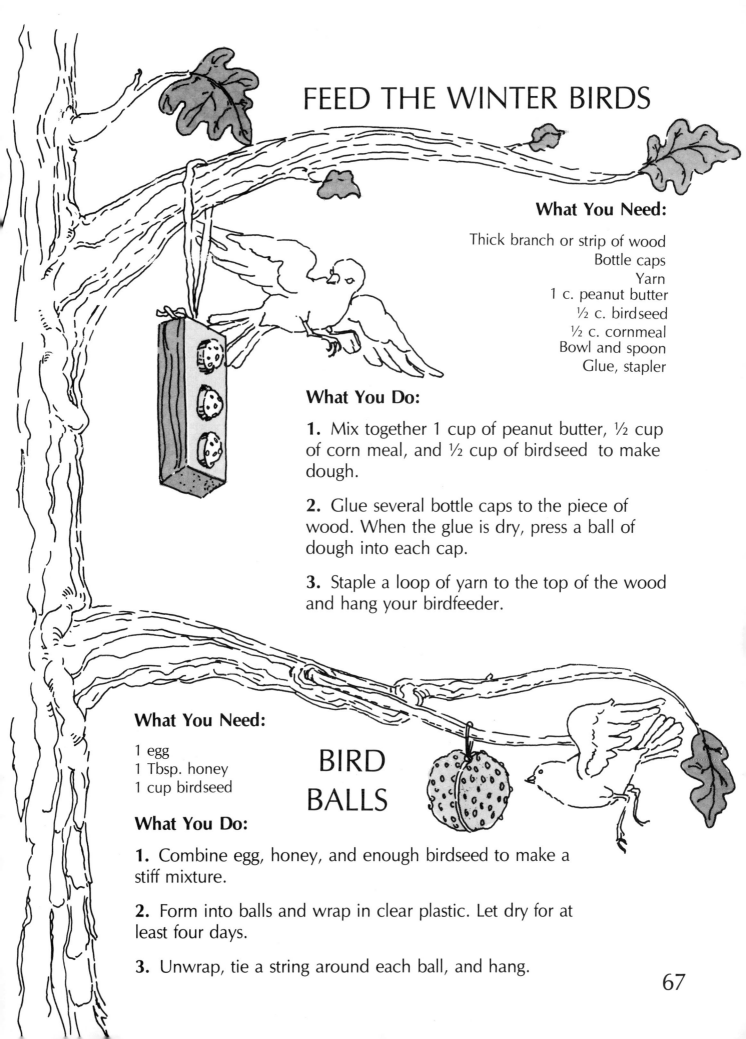

FEED THE WINTER BIRDS

What You Need:

Thick branch or strip of wood
Bottle caps
Yarn
1 c. peanut butter
½ c. birdseed
½ c. cornmeal
Bowl and spoon
Glue, stapler

What You Do:

1. Mix together 1 cup of peanut butter, ½ cup of corn meal, and ½ cup of birdseed to make dough.

2. Glue several bottle caps to the piece of wood. When the glue is dry, press a ball of dough into each cap.

3. Staple a loop of yarn to the top of the wood and hang your birdfeeder.

What You Need:

1 egg
1 Tbsp. honey
1 cup birdseed

BIRD BALLS

What You Do:

1. Combine egg, honey, and enough birdseed to make a stiff mixture.

2. Form into balls and wrap in clear plastic. Let dry for at least four days.

3. Unwrap, tie a string around each ball, and hang.

67

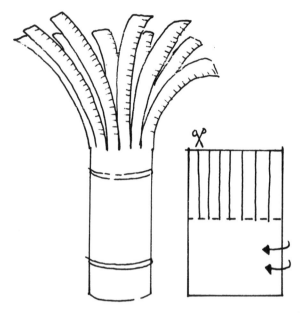

LEAFY PALM TREE

What You Do:

1. Fold paper in half. Color the top half green on both sides and the bottom half on one side only. Cut slits down the top half, stopping at the fold.

2. Roll the paper and fasten with 2 rubber bands. Notch the strips and curl each green strip around your finger or a crayon.

What You Need:

Large sheet of paper
Crayons, markers, or paint
Scissors
2 rubber bands

A BLOOMING ALMOND TREE

What You Need:

Long cardboard roll
Cotton balls
Red or pink chalk
Green tissue paper
Paper plate
Scissors, glue

Chalk

Cotton balls

What You Do:

1. Cut strips halfway down the cardboard roll to form branches. Spread apart.

2. Rub the chalk on the paper plate to make chalk dust. Roll cotton balls on the dust until they turn pink. Glue them on the branches.

3. Crinkle small pieces of green tissue to make leaves. Glue them on the branches, too.

A TREE THAT GROWS

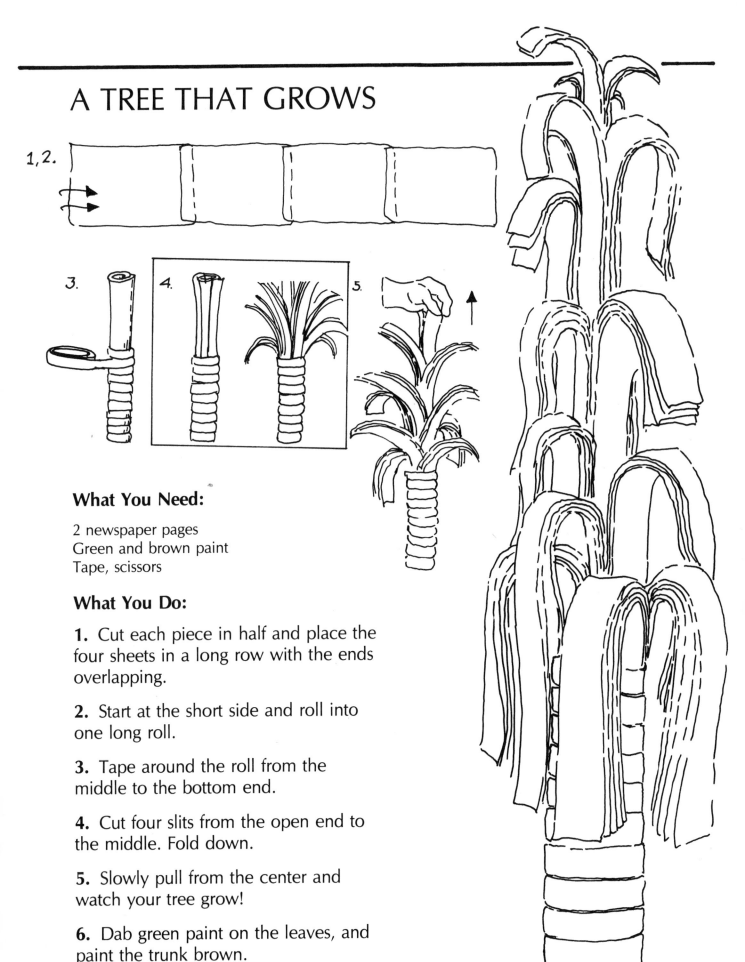

What You Need:

2 newspaper pages
Green and brown paint
Tape, scissors

What You Do:

1. Cut each piece in half and place the four sheets in a long row with the ends overlapping.

2. Start at the short side and roll into one long roll.

3. Tape around the roll from the middle to the bottom end.

4. Cut four slits from the open end to the middle. Fold down.

5. Slowly pull from the center and watch your tree grow!

6. Dab green paint on the leaves, and paint the trunk brown.

69

ORANGE TREE

What You Need:

Brown paper bag
Old newspapers
Long cardboard roll
Rubber band
Colored paper
Decorating scraps
Glue, scissors

What You Do:

1. Put the cardboard roll in the center of the open paper bag to form a trunk. Crush the newspapers into balls and stuff them all around the trunk.

2. Close the bag around the trunk and fasten with a rubber band.

3. Cover the trunk with dark paper and fabric scraps. Use colorful scraps to decorate the tree with leaves and fruit.

70

TU B'SHEVAT CENTERPIECE

What You Need:

Long cardboard roll
Paint
Paper plate
Decorating scraps
Scissors, glue

What You Do:

1. Make two slits in the top of the cardboard roll. Paint the roll black or brown.

2. Decorate both sides of a large paper plate with leaves and pictures of your favorite fruit. Use paint, paper, or fabric scraps.

3. Push the plate into the slits in the cardboard roll.

A THREE-SIDED ORANGE TREE

What You Need:

Three sheets of paper
Scissors, glue
Tissue paper
Crayons

What You Do:

1. Put three sheets of paper together and fold them in half. Draw half a tree along the fold and cut out.

2. Write the number "1" on half of each tree and the number "2" on the other half. Paste each "1" part to the "2" part of a different tree.

3. Draw oranges on your tree with crayons, or glue on bits of orange tissue paper.

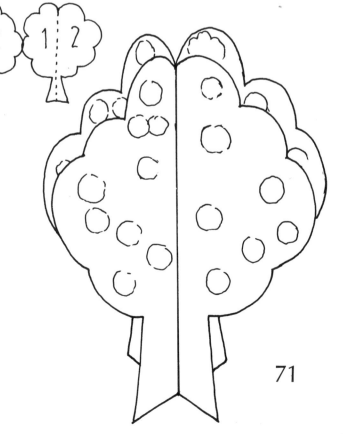

71

TREE CERTIFICATE FRAME

What You Need:

Large paper bag
Yarn
8 paper clips
Scissors, pencil

What You Do:

1. Choose a paper bag with a bottom slightly larger than your tree certificate. Put a mark 2 fingers wide on each corner of the bottom of the bag.

2. Cut down each side to the marks.

3. Roll each section tightly as far as you can. Put paper clips on each end to hold the rolls.

4. Glue the tree certificate to the center of the frame.

5. Push yarn through the top roll and tie a loop. The frame is ready to hang.

WATERING CAN TZEDAKAH BOX

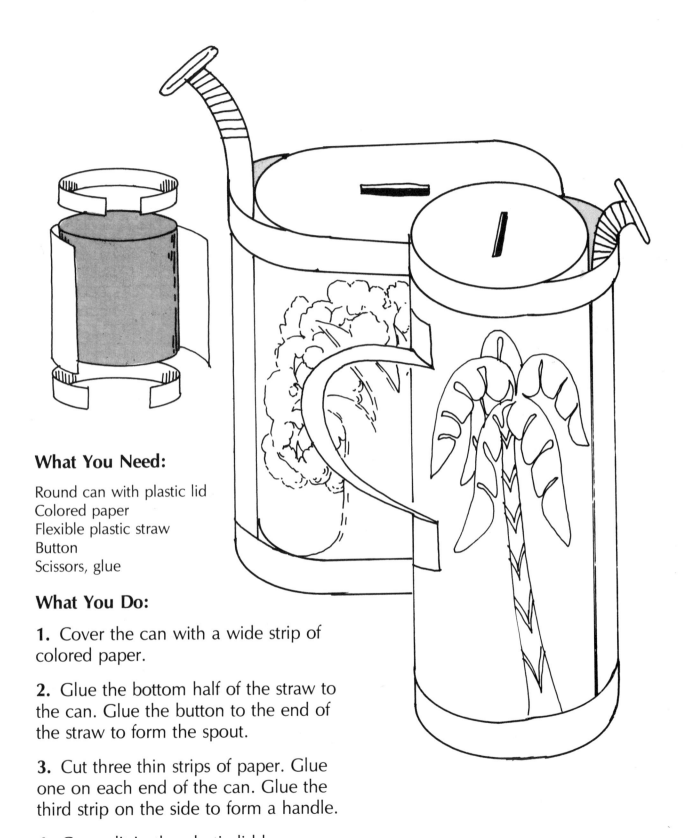

What You Need:

Round can with plastic lid
Colored paper
Flexible plastic straw
Button
Scissors, glue

What You Do:

1. Cover the can with a wide strip of colored paper.

2. Glue the bottom half of the straw to the can. Glue the button to the end of the straw to form the spout.

3. Cut three thin strips of paper. Glue one on each end of the can. Glue the third strip on the side to form a handle.

4. Cut a slit in the plastic lid large enough for coins.

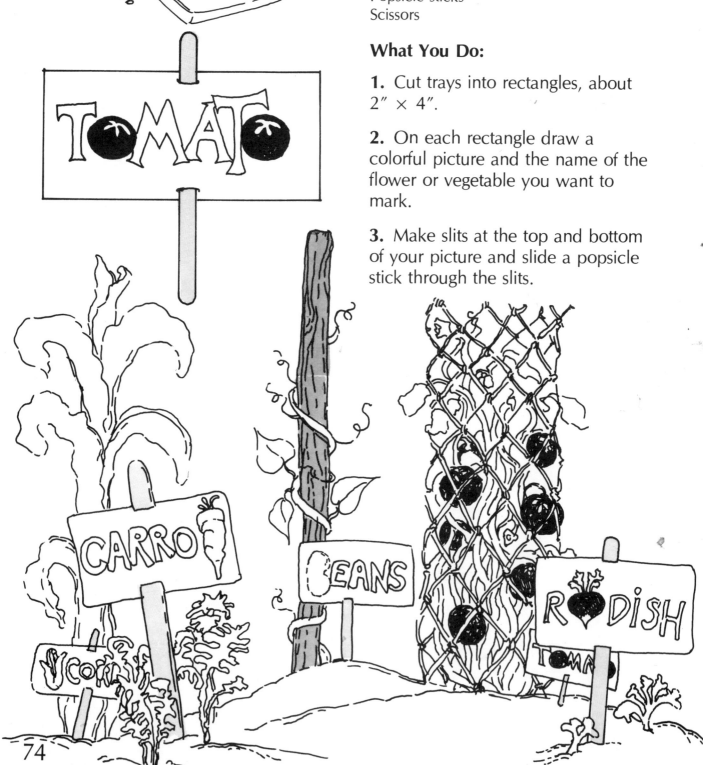

What You Need:

Meat trays
Waterproof markers
Popsicle sticks
Scissors

What You Do:

1. Cut trays into rectangles, about 2" × 4".

2. On each rectangle draw a colorful picture and the name of the flower or vegetable you want to mark.

3. Make slits at the top and bottom of your picture and slide a popsicle stick through the slits.

74

GROWING THINGS

SWEET POTATO VINE

What You Need:

Sweet potato
Toothpicks
Glass of water

Put four toothpicks around the center of a sweet potato and balance it in a glass of water. About half your potato should be in the water. In a few days roots will form and about a week later leaves will begin to grow.

CARROT AND TURNIP TOPS

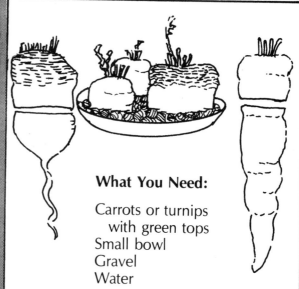

What You Need:

Carrots or turnips
    with green tops
Small bowl
Gravel
Water

Cut about an inch off the tops of several carrots and turnips. Put a layer of gravel in the bowl. Put the carrot and turnip tops in the bowl. Add water. It will take about a week before you see the little green tops begin to grow.

WATCH A BEAN SPROUT

What You Need:

Small jar
Cotton or tissues
Dried lima beans

Put cotton or tissues in a glass jar. Place several lima beans around the edges. Sprinkle with water and keep moist. In just a few days you will see the roots begin to grow.

CITRUS SPROUTERS

What You Need:

Paper cups, potting soil, dish
Grapefruit, lemon, or orange seeds

Punch holes in the bottom of a paper cup and fill it with potting soil. Place a few seeds in each cup and cover with a thin layer of soil. Put the cups on small dishes and place them on a sunny window sill. Keep the soil moist. These seeds take awhile to grow, so be patient.

PURIM

Come to the Megillah reading, and hear how brave Queen Esther saved the Jewish people of Persia from wicked Haman's evil plot to kill them. Twirl your grogger so you can't hear Haman's name. Let's celebrate with merry-making and parades, gifts to the poor, and sweet treats for our friends.

WORDS TO KNOW

Purim — Festival of Lots, named for the magic numbers used by Haman to choose a day to kill the Jews

Megillah — scroll of the story of Queen Esther

Grogger — noisemaker — the Hebrew word is "ra'ashan"

Hamantaschen — filled cookie; the word means "Haman's pockets"

Shalach Manot — the exchange of cookies, fruit, and other treats among friends and neighbors; the words mean "sending gifts"

Queen Esther — Jewish heroine

Mordecai — Esther's cousin

Haman — wicked prime minister of Persia

King Ahashuerus — ruler of Persia

PURIM

PURIM PARADERS

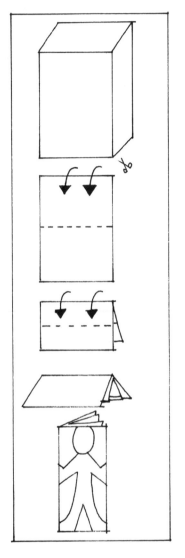

What You Need:

Large paper bag or large piece of paper
Scissors, glue
Crayons and decorating scraps

What You Do:

1. Cut out one side of a large paper bag. Fold it in half and in half again in the same direction.

2. Draw the shape of a person. Make sure the arms reach the edges. When you cut out the people, be careful not to cut the arms along the fold. Unfold.

3. With crayons and decorating scraps, create a different costume for each parader.

POP-UP FACE PUPPETS

What You Need:

4 paper cups
4 plastic straws
Construction paper
Egg carton lid
Markers, scissors, glue

What You Do:

1. On a sheet of white construction paper, trace around the bottom of a cup four times. Cut out the circles for your puppet faces.

2. Use markers and colored paper to make the Purim characters. Don't forget Queen Esther's crown and Haman's 3-cornered hat.

3. Glue each puppet face to a plastic straw.

4. Glue the four cups to the egg carton lid. After they are dry, punch a hole through the lid into each cup.

5. Push the straws through the holes, so puppets are hidden inside the cups. Make each puppet pop up as you tell the story of Purim.

BALLOON FACES

What You Need:

Balloons
Decorating scraps
Markers, tape, string

What You Do:

1. Blow up balloons and knot them.

2. Decorate with markers and scraps.
Hang your balloon faces.

STICK PUPPETS

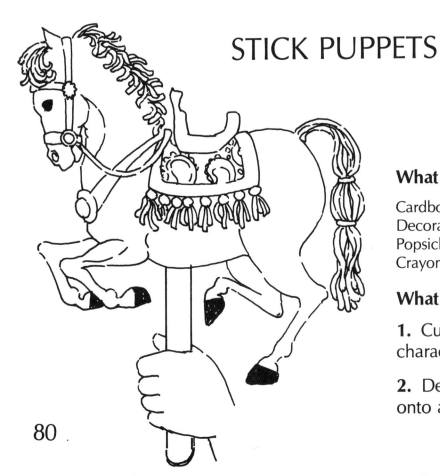

What You Need:

Cardboard
Decorating scraps
Popsicle sticks
Crayons, markers, scissors, glue

What You Do:

1. Cut out and color Purim characters.

2. Decorate and glue each figure onto a popsicle stick.

RIDE THE KING'S HORSE

What You Need:

3 large paper bags
Old sock
Newspaper
Yarn, buttons, markers
Glue, scissors, rubber bands

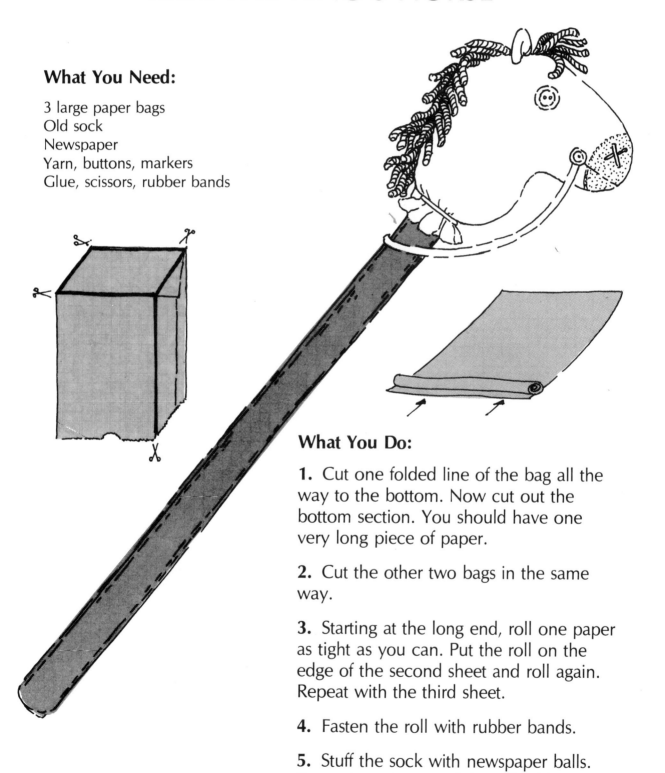

What You Do:

1. Cut one folded line of the bag all the way to the bottom. Now cut out the bottom section. You should have one very long piece of paper.

2. Cut the other two bags in the same way.

3. Starting at the long end, roll one paper as tight as you can. Put the roll on the edge of the second sheet and roll again. Repeat with the third sheet.

4. Fasten the roll with rubber bands.

5. Stuff the sock with newspaper balls. Fasten it to the top of the roll with a rubber band. Decorate the horse's head with yarn, buttons, and markers.

QUICK AND EASY ROBE

What You Need:

2 large paper bags
Paint, scissors, glue, stapler
Yarn, decorating scraps
Towel

What You Do:

1. Cut out the bottom of a large paper bag. Cut two narrow strips from the second paper bag long enough to fit over your shoulders. Glue or staple the straps to the first paper bag.

2. Paint and decorate the robe. Add a belt made from several long pieces of yarn.

3. Top your costume off with a colorful towel cape!

ANOTHER ROYAL ROBE

What You Need:

Large paper bag
Paint, crayons, markers
Decorating scraps
Pipe cleaners
Scissors, glue, hole punch

What You Do:

1. Cut a line down the center of one of the big sides of the bag from the top to the bottom.

2. Cut a hole out of the bottom of the bag large enough to fit over your head. Try it on to make sure!

3. Cut armholes from each side section of the bag. Try these, too.

4. Punch holes along each of the open sides. Use pipe cleaners to ''button up.''

5. Decorate your costume with markers and scraps. For Mordecai, be sure to wear a kippah. For Haman, make a cardboard sword to tuck under your belt. For Queen Esther, add a cardboard crown and jewels.

83

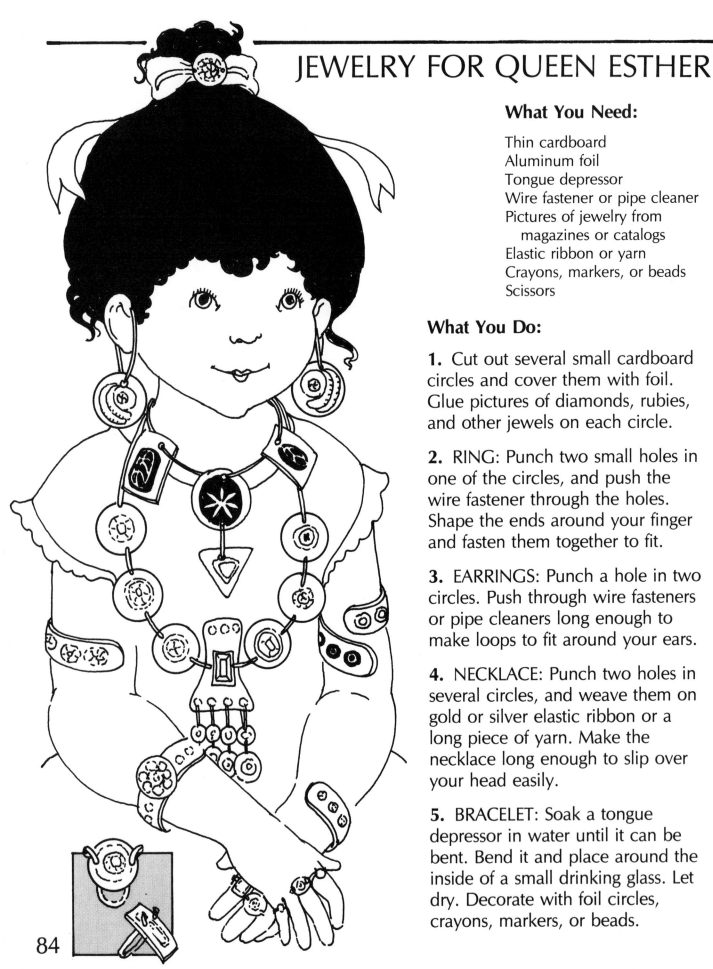

JEWELRY FOR QUEEN ESTHER

What You Need:

Thin cardboard
Aluminum foil
Tongue depressor
Wire fastener or pipe cleaner
Pictures of jewelry from
    magazines or catalogs
Elastic ribbon or yarn
Crayons, markers, or beads
Scissors

What You Do:

1. Cut out several small cardboard circles and cover them with foil. Glue pictures of diamonds, rubies, and other jewels on each circle.

2. RING: Punch two small holes in one of the circles, and push the wire fastener through the holes. Shape the ends around your finger and fasten them together to fit.

3. EARRINGS: Punch a hole in two circles. Push through wire fasteners or pipe cleaners long enough to make loops to fit around your ears.

4. NECKLACE: Punch two holes in several circles, and weave them on gold or silver elastic ribbon or a long piece of yarn. Make the necklace long enough to slip over your head easily.

5. BRACELET: Soak a tongue depressor in water until it can be bent. Bend it and place around the inside of a small drinking glass. Let dry. Decorate with foil circles, crayons, markers, or beads.

84

CROWN

MASK

What You Need:

Large paper bag
Scissors, stapler, glue
Decorating scraps

What You Do:

1. Cut a large circle from one panel of a paper bag.

2. Fold the circle in half. Cut five slits, starting at the centerfold each time. Do not cut all the way to the edge.

3. Unfold and place on your head. If the opening is too small, refold and cut slits a little longer.

4. Fold each cut triangle down and staple to the outside rim. Fold end points of each triangle upward.

5. Decorate the crown.

What You Need:

2 large paper plates
Scissors
Decorating scraps, cotton balls, paper

What You Do:

1. Cut out a large circle from the center of one plate. The outer ring should slip over your head easily. If it does not, cut a little more. Staple the top of the ring to another plate.

2. Cut out eyes. Add a nose and mouth, hair or hat, and decorate your mask.

GIVE HAMAN A HEADACHE

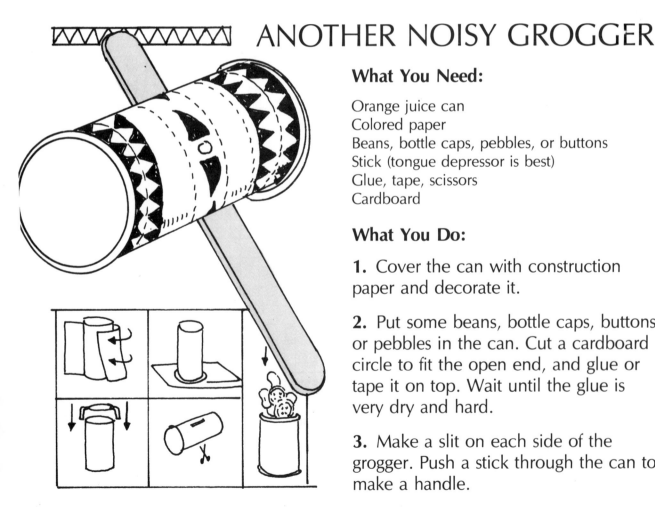

What You Need:

Small paper plate
Dried beans
Stapler
Popsicle stick
Crayons or markers
Decorating scraps

What You Do:

1. Fold the paper plate in half. Put some dried beans inside and staple the plate shut. Staple a popsicle stick to the plate to make a handle.

2. Draw or paint Haman's face on the folded plate. Add decorating scraps for his hat, beard, and moustache.

ANOTHER NOISY GROGGER

What You Need:

Orange juice can
Colored paper
Beans, bottle caps, pebbles, or buttons
Stick (tongue depressor is best)
Glue, tape, scissors
Cardboard

What You Do:

1. Cover the can with construction paper and decorate it.

2. Put some beans, bottle caps, buttons, or pebbles in the can. Cut a cardboard circle to fit the open end, and glue or tape it on top. Wait until the glue is very dry and hard.

3. Make a slit on each side of the grogger. Push a stick through the can to make a handle.

HOOT HAMAN

What You Need:

Cardboard roll
Waxed paper
Rubber band
Colored paper
Fat nail
Scissors, yarn

What You Do:

1. Cover one end of the roll with waxed paper and attach with a rubber band.

2. Cover the roll with colored paper. Use the nail to poke four air holes on one side.

3. Make two more holes near the bottom edge, and attach a loop of yarn so you may wear the Purim noisemaker.

TAMBOURINE

What You Need:

2 paper plates
Crayons or decorating scraps
Hole punch
8 bottle caps
Hammer and nail
Wire or plastic bag ties
Glue

What You Do:

1. Decorate the insides of two paper plates. Hold them with the blank sides together and punch four holes evenly around both plates. Glue.

2. Punch a hole in the bottle caps with a hammer and nail. Fasten two bottle caps with wire through each set of holes.

87

SHALACH MANOT BASKETS

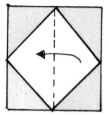 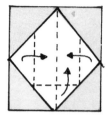 

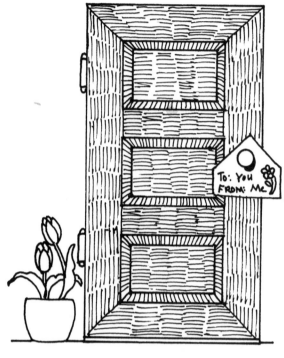

What You Need:

Large paper square
Decorating scraps and markers
Scissors, glue, tape

What You Do:

1. Turn the paper square so it looks like a diamond. Fold the diamond in half sideways and unfold it.

2. Fold each side to the center fold. Fold the bottom point up to meet the side points. Glue or tape them together.

3. Decorate the basket with scraps, and write TO, FROM, and a Purim greeting.

4. Cut out a hole near the top point. If your friends are away when you arrive, you may hang the basket on the doorknob.

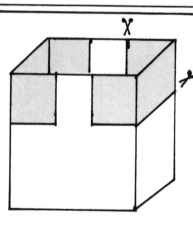

What You Need:

Empty milk carton
Colored paper
    or paint mixed
    with liquid detergent
Decorating scraps
Scissors, glue, stapler

What You Do:

1. Cut down a milk carton as shown in the picture. Staple the handle together.

2. Paint the basket or cover it with colored paper. Decorate with scraps or draw Purim designs.

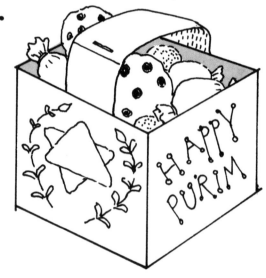

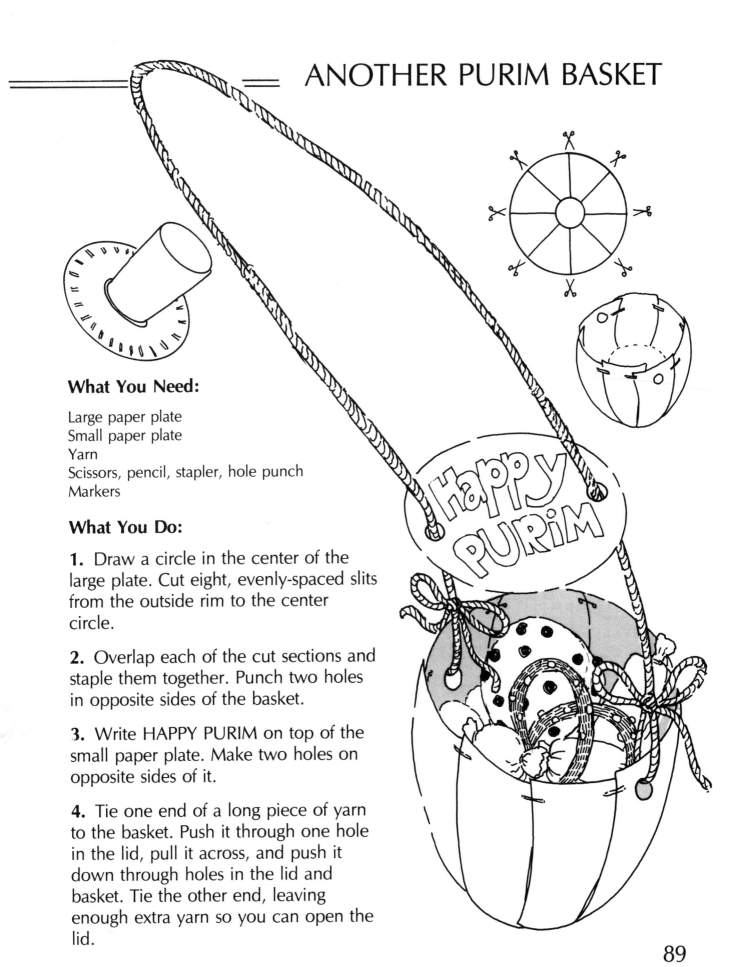

ANOTHER PURIM BASKET

What You Need:

Large paper plate
Small paper plate
Yarn
Scissors, pencil, stapler, hole punch
Markers

What You Do:

1. Draw a circle in the center of the large plate. Cut eight, evenly-spaced slits from the outside rim to the center circle.

2. Overlap each of the cut sections and staple them together. Punch two holes in opposite sides of the basket.

3. Write HAPPY PURIM on top of the small paper plate. Make two holes on opposite sides of it.

4. Tie one end of a long piece of yarn to the basket. Push it through one hole in the lid, pull it across, and push it down through holes in the lid and basket. Tie the other end, leaving enough extra yarn so you can open the lid.

PASSOVER

We gather at the seder table and retell in story and song how the Jewish people were freed from slavery in Egypt. The matzah reminds us that our ancestors left Egypt in haste; the maror, how bitter is the life of a slave. We recline on pillows, happy to live in a land of freedom.

WORDS TO KNOW

Passover — spring holiday celebrating the exodus from Egypt. The Hebrew name is "Pesach".

Seder — Passover family meal at which we recount the story of the Exodus

Seder Plate — dish containing symbolic seder foods: parsley, bitter herbs, egg, bone, and charoset

Matzah — flat, unleavened bread

Afikomen — special matzah hidden at the seder to amuse children

Cup of Elijah — special cup of wine set aside for the prophet Elijah, who is said to visit each seder

Charoset — chopped apples and nuts that recall the mortar used by Jewish slaves to make bricks

Maror — bitter herbs

Four Questions — questions about the story of Passover asked by the youngest at the seder

Moses — Jewish leader who took his people out of Egypt

PASSOVER

FORSYTHIA FLOWERS FOR THE SEDER TABLE

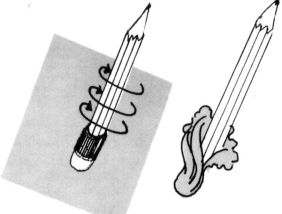

What You Need:

Plastic box from fruits or vegetables
2 paper napkins
Yellow tissue paper
Plastic straws
Jar lid
Pencil, scissors, glue

What You Do:

1. Cut small squares of tissue. Place the eraser end of a pencil in the center of each square, and twist the paper around the pencil.

2. Pour a small amount of glue in the jar lid. Dip the tissue covered pencil into the glue, then stick it on top of a plastic straw and carefully remove the pencil.

3. Fluff the napkins into balls, and stuff them in the vegetable box.

4. Turn the box over, and push the straws through the holes in the box so the flowers will stand in the vase.

SEDER PLATE

What You Need:

Paper plate
Colored paper
Small muffin cups
Scissors, crayons, glue

What You Do:

1. Draw and cut out pictures of a bone, an egg, a green vegetable (lettuce, parsley, or celery), a bowl of charoset, and bitter horseradish. Glue the pictures around the edges of a large paper plate. Next to each picture glue a small muffin cup.

2. Before the seder, put the real food into each muffin cup, and put the plate on your seder table. On the second night of Passover, you can replace the muffin cups with new ones.

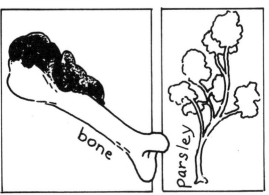
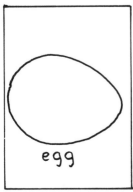

bone

parsley

egg

charoset

horseradish

MATZAH COVER

What You Need:

Four pieces of colored paper larger than a matzah
Yarn
Colored tissue paper
Crayons
Scissors, glue, hole punch
Small bowl of water

What You Do:

1. Put the four pieces of paper together and punch holes around three sides. Fasten a piece of yarn at one end, sew loosely around to the other end, and fasten.

2. Write the word "Matzah" on the cover. Cut shapes from different colored tissue paper. Place them on the cover, wet them with your finger, and take them off. Surprise! The colors stay on the paper.

94

TIE-DYE AFIKOMEN CLOTH

What You Need:

Food coloring
3 small bowls
Large white handkerchief, napkin, or piece of cloth
Crayons

What You Do:

1. Write the word AFIKOMEN in the middle of the cloth. Press hard with the crayon. Draw Passover designs around the edges.

2. Put a cup of water in each bowl. Add a few drops of a different food coloring to each bowl.

3. Twist a corner of the cloth and dip it into one color. Squeeze it dry. Twist another corner and dip it into a different color. Squeeze it dry. Keep twisting and dipping and squeezing until the cloth is covered. Dry flat.

AFIKOMEN BAG

What You Need:

2 pieces of fabric (slightly larger than half a matzah)
Needle and yarn
Decorating scraps
Markers, scissors, glue

What You Do:

1. Write "AFIKOMEN" on one piece of fabric and decorate with scraps.

2. Sew the two pieces together on three sides.

3. Weave the yarn in and out of the open edges, leaving enough on each end for a drawstring. Knot each end.

MATZAH TRAY

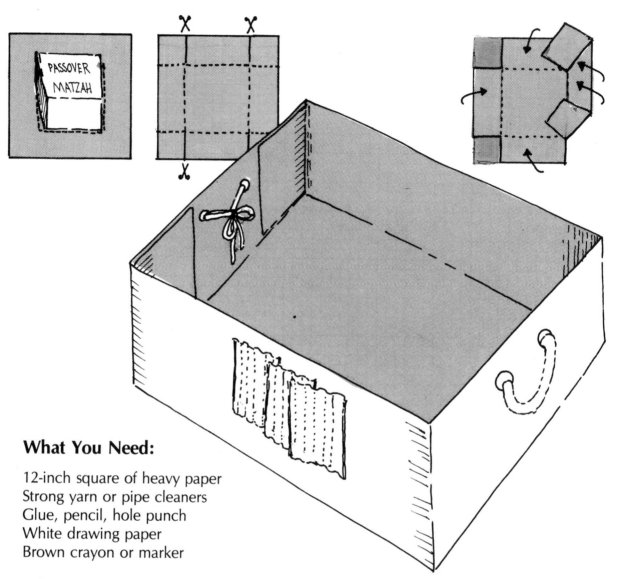

What You Need:

12-inch square of heavy paper
Strong yarn or pipe cleaners
Glue, pencil, hole punch
White drawing paper
Brown crayon or marker

What You Do:

1. Place a box of matzah in the middle of the paper and trace around it. Turn the paper over so the lines are on the bottom. Fold up the sides to the lines.

2. Cut one slit up to the fold line at each corner. Glue the side flaps inside.

3. Punch two holes on two sides of the tray and attach yarn or pipe cleaners to make handles.

4. Draw and cut out small squares of paper. Decorate them to look like matzah, and glue them to the sides of the tray.

SEDER PILLOW

What You Need:

Long rectangle of strong paper (shelf paper or cut-up grocery bag)
Old newspapers
Colored paper
Scissors, glue, markers, stapler

What You Do:

1. Fold the paper rectangle almost in half, leaving a short flap on one end. Staple the sides closed.

2. Crumple up newspaper balls and stuff them inside to make a fat pillow. Put glue on the flap and fold it down to close the pillow. Glue a folded strip of colored paper along each side to cover the staples.

3. Decorate with markers and colored paper shapes.

97

HAGGADAH BOOKMARK

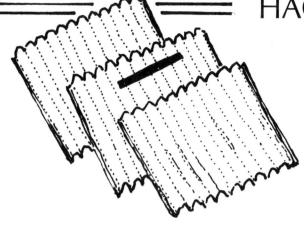

What You Do:

1. Draw a design of three matzot, cut it out, and color it. Cut a slit in the middle matzah.

2. To mark your place, push the page corner through the slit.

What You Need:

Thin cardboard
Brown crayon or marker
Scissors

WINE-SIPPER PLACECARDS

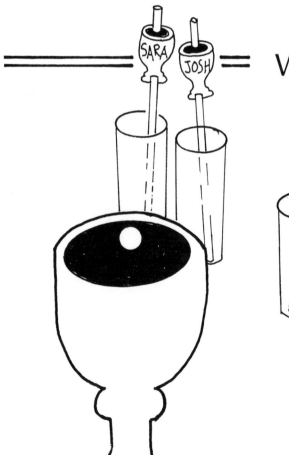

What You Need:

Construction paper
Straws
Scissors, hole punch, markers

What You Do:

1. Draw a small wine cup and cut it out. Write your guest's name and decorate.

2. Punch holes near the top and bottom.

3. Push a straw through the holes. Make enough wine sippers for everyone at your seder.

Hint: You can trace this cup and cut out several at a time!

What You Need:

Labels from Passover foods (matzah, wine, gefilte fish, etc.)
Construction paper
Clear self-adhesive shelf paper
Scissors, glue

What You Do:

1. Arrange the labels in a collage on a piece of construction paper. Glue down.

2. Cover on both sides with adhesive paper.

3. The placemats may be wiped clean and stored for future holiday meals.

WINE TRAY

What You Need:

Styrofoam tray
Jar lid
Paper towel
Purple, green, and brown paint
Clear adhesive paper

What You Do:

1. Fold up the paper towel and put it in the jar lid. Soak the towel with purple paint.

2. Dip your pinky on the paint pad and then press it on the tray. Make groups of purple pinky prints to look like bunches of grapes. Paint brown stems and green leaves.

3. When the paint is dry, cover the tray with clear adhesive paper.

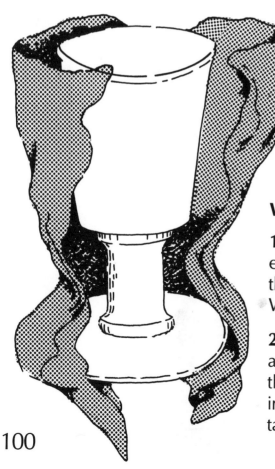

ELIJAH'S GOBLET

What You Need:

Cardboard egg carton
Empty spool
2 paper cups
Aluminum foil
Scissors, glue

What You Do:

1. Draw a big circle on the top of a cardboard egg carton. Cut it out. Glue an empty spool to the circle and glue a paper cup to the spool. Wait until the glue is very dry.

2. Cover the cup, stem, and base with aluminum foil. Squeeze the foil carefully around the stem. Fill the second cup with wine, place it in the silver goblet, and put it on your seder table.

MOSES IN THE BASKET

What You Need:

Egg carton lid
Aluminum foil
Cotton balls
Fabric
Clothespin
Scissors, glue, markers

What You Do:

1. Cut the egg carton lid in half. Cover it with aluminum foil. Build the foil up along the cut side, so that is even with the other sides.

2. Glue cotton balls to line the inside of the lid.

3. Cut fabric to fit inside the lid. Put glue along the sides and gently press the blanket fabric on the cotton lining.

4. Use the clothespin for Baby Moses. Draw his face with markers. Tuck him under the blanket.

FOUR QUESTION REMINDER

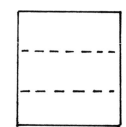

What You Need:

Colored paper
Scissors, glue, markers

What You Do:

1. Fold a large piece of colored paper into thirds. Open to make a triangular standing sign.

2. Fold another piece of colored paper in half and in half again. Cut out a large question-mark shape through all the folds. Glue the four question marks onto the sign.

3. Cut out four white circles. Draw a piece of matzah on the first circle. Draw a bitter vegetable on the second circle. Draw two bowls on the third circle. Draw a chair with a pillow on the fourth circle.

4. Glue your circles under each question mark.

Now your sign will help you remember The Four Questions!

1. Why do we eat only matzah at Passover?
2. Why do we taste a bitter vegetable?
3. Why do we dip twice?
4. Why do we sit back and relax?

CHAROSET

What You Need:
Apples
Walnuts
Passover wine or grape juice
Bowl, knife, peeler, nutcracker

What You Do:

1. Peel and cut two apples into tiny chunks. Shell the nuts and cut into small pieces. Add to apples.

2. Add enough wine to moisten. Mix well and refrigerate.

UNSANDWICHES

APPLE

Cut an apple into wedges. Discard core. Spread with cream cheese and top with jelly.

WALNUT

Add ¼ tsp. brown sugar and ½ c. raisins to 3 oz. softened cream cheese. Spread some on half a walnut and cover with other half.

BANANA

Peel banana and slice the long way. Spread one slice with jam and cover. Cut into bite-sized pieces.

YOM HA'ATZMAUT _____

Happy Birthday, Israel! On this day in 1948, Israel's first Prime Minister, David Ben Gurion, proclaimed the creation of the new state. Dance the hora, sing Hatikvah, and join the parades. We're proud of the pioneers who settled in Israel and the brave soldiers who defend her.

WORDS TO KNOW

Yom Ha'atzmaut — Day of Independence

Mizrach — plaque placed on the eastern wall of a home, facing Jerusalem, the capital of Israel; the word means "east"

Israel — homeland of the Jewish people

Hora — Israeli folk dance

Hatikvah — Israel's national anthem

YOM HA'ATZMAUT

WALK-A-THON BACKSACK

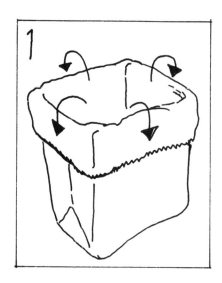

What You Need:

Sturdy paper bag
2 old neckties or strong yarn
Colored paper
Scissors, markers, glue

What You Do:

1. Open the paper bag. Fold over a flap all around the top. Now fold it over again.

2. On one wide side of the bag, cut two small holes on the flap near each corner and two small holes below them near the bottom. Push an old necktie or heavy yarn through each pair of holes. Tie the ends together so the backsack fits you.

3. Decorate the sack with special designs for Israel's birthday.

BIRTHDAY FAN FOR ISRAEL

What You Need:

2 paper plates
Large cardboard roll
Old magazine or colored paper
Scissors, glue, markers

What You Do:

1. Glue the rims of the paper plates together, front to front.

2. Cut two deep slits in the cardboard roll. Push the plates into the slits. Put glue along the slits to hold the plates tight.

3. Cut out big letters I S R A E L from a magazine, or make them from colored paper. Glue them on one side of the fan. Glue Israel's birthday numbers on the other side.

4. Draw colorful balloon shapes around each letter and number. Draw wiggly strings from each balloon to the fan handle.

A STAR IN A CIRCLE

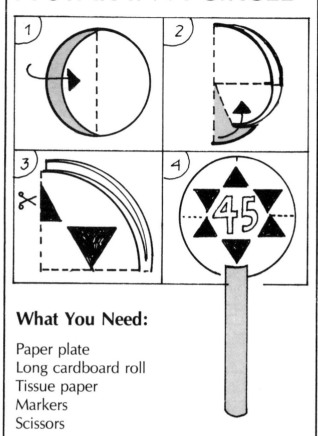

What You Need:

Paper plate
Long cardboard roll
Tissue paper
Markers
Scissors

What You Do:

1. Roll tissue paper around the cardboard roll and tuck in the ends. Cut two slits at the top of one end.

2. Fold the plate in half and in half again.

3. Cut a triangle from the center of the side that has one fold. The point of the triangle should be at the fold. Now cut a second triangle from the side that has two folds. Make one side nearly touch the base of the first triangle.

4. Open the plate. Write Israel's birthday number in the center and decorate. Slide the plate into the slits of the roll.

STAR MOBILE

What You Need:

Blue and white colored paper
Coat hanger
Glue, scissors, string

What You Do:

1. Cut one white and six blue paper circles. Fold the six blue ones in half, and cut each one from the center of the fold halfway to the edge.

2. Push the blue circles around the white one to form the shape of a Jewish star. Glue or tape the edges together.

3. Make several stars and tie them to strings of different lengths. Hang your stars from a coat hanger to create a star mobile.

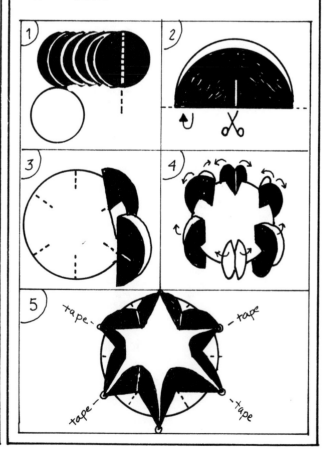

KIBBUTZ TRACTOR

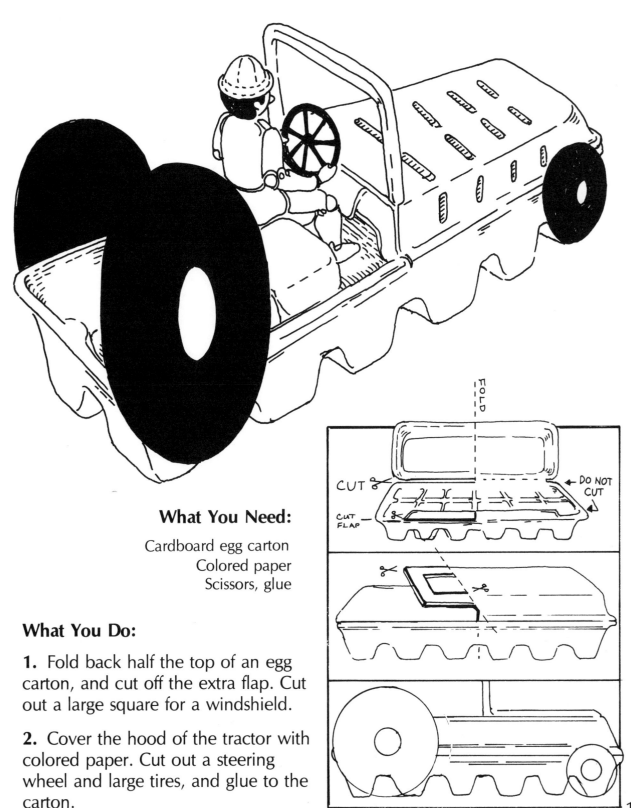

What You Need:

Cardboard egg carton
Colored paper
Scissors, glue

What You Do:

1. Fold back half the top of an egg carton, and cut off the extra flap. Cut out a large square for a windshield.

2. Cover the hood of the tractor with colored paper. Cut out a steering wheel and large tires, and glue to the carton.

109

MIZRACH PLAQUE

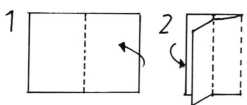

What You Need:

1 sheet colored paper
1 sheet white paper
Scissors, glue, crayons

What You Do:

1. Fold a piece of paper in half horizontally, and in half again in the same direction.

2. Draw or trace the shape of a palm tree along the closed fold. Cut it out.

3. Open carefully and write the Hebrew letters for mizrach. Decorate.

4. Paste your paper cut over a sheet of colored paper and hang it on an eastern wall.

MILK AND HONEY COOKIES

What You Need:

¼ c. peanut butter
¼ c. honey
½ c. powdered milk
Powdered sugar
Bowls

What You Do:

1. Put peanut butter, honey, and powdered milk into a bowl and mix well. The batter will be stiff.

2. Form the dough into little balls and roll them in a dish of powdered sugar.

LAG B'OMER _____

The seven weeks between Passover and Shavuot are called the Omer, named for the sheaves of wheat brought to the Holy Temple each day. Lag B'Omer is the 33rd day of the Omer. When the Romans ruled Israel, Torah study was forbidden. The great teacher, Shimon Bar Yochai, hid in a cave. Each spring on Lag B'Omer, his students came to see him, dressed as hunters to fool the enemy. Today it has become an outdoor celebration, with picnics, hikes, and sports events.

WORDS TO KNOW

Lag B'Omer — 33rd day of the Omer. Hebrew letters stand for numbers. The letters L (lamed) and G (gimmel) equal 33.

Shimon Bar Yochai — Second Century scholar of mysticism who fled the Romans and hid in a cave with his son for 12 years.

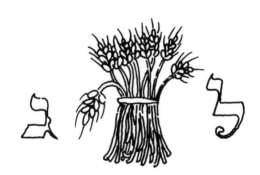

LAG B'OMER

PAPER BAG KITE

What You Need:

Small paper bag
Colored paper
String, stapler
Scissors, glue, markers

What You Do:

1. Fold over a band at the top of the bag. Fold over again to make it stronger.

2. Cut out a big circle from the closed end of the bag and discard.

3. Cut long, thin strips of colored paper and glue them around the open circle. Decorate.

4. Staple the ends of a very long string to the open edges of the bag.

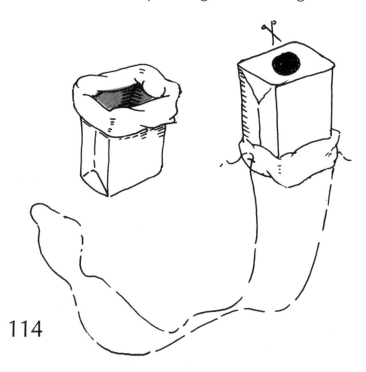

114

SUN HAT

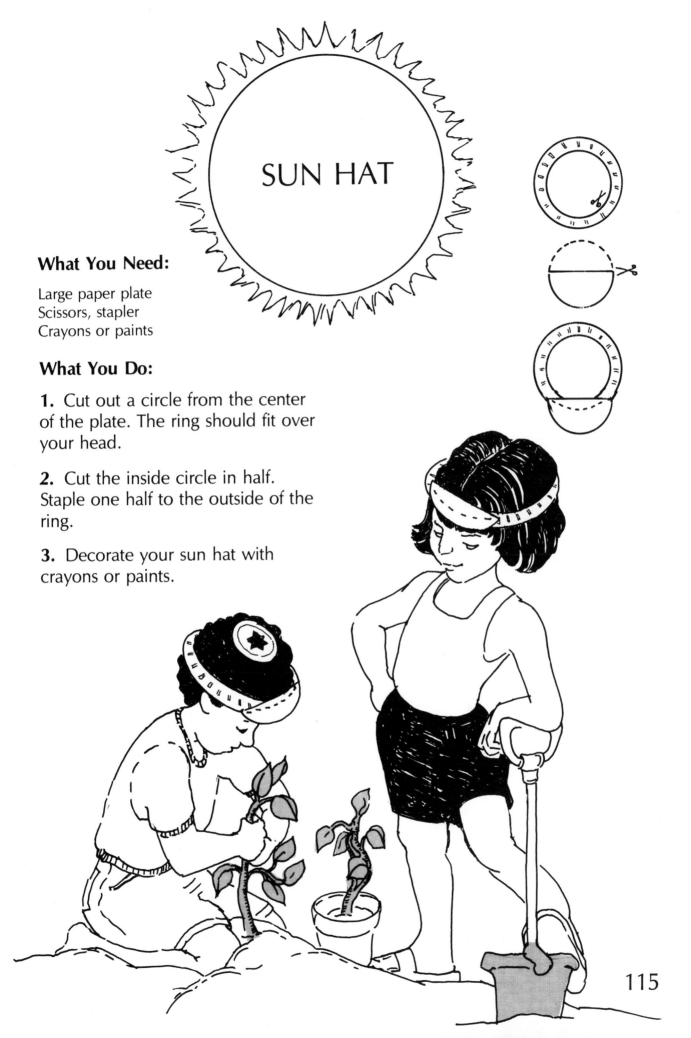

What You Need:

Large paper plate
Scissors, stapler
Crayons or paints

What You Do:

1. Cut out a circle from the center of the plate. The ring should fit over your head.

2. Cut the inside circle in half. Staple one half to the outside of the ring.

3. Decorate your sun hat with crayons or paints.

STAR OF DAVID PINWHEEL

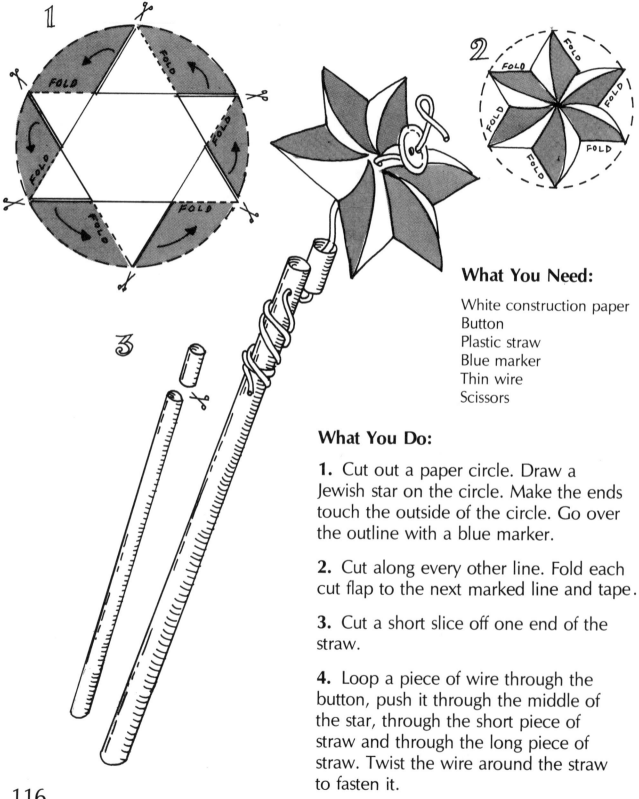

What You Need:

White construction paper
Button
Plastic straw
Blue marker
Thin wire
Scissors

What You Do:

1. Cut out a paper circle. Draw a Jewish star on the circle. Make the ends touch the outside of the circle. Go over the outline with a blue marker.

2. Cut along every other line. Fold each cut flap to the next marked line and tape.

3. Cut a short slice off one end of the straw.

4. Loop a piece of wire through the button, push it through the middle of the star, through the short piece of straw and through the long piece of straw. Twist the wire around the straw to fasten it.

BOX LUNCH

What You Need:

Egg carton
Decorating scraps, ribbon,
    glue
Finger foods

What You Do:

1. Decorate the top of an egg carton, and fill with finger foods — cheese cubes, cut-up fruit, berries, carrot and celery sticks, hard-cooked eggs, cookies, etc.

2. Close and tie with ribbon or yarn. Refrigerate if necessary.

LUNCH TOTE

What You Need:

Oatmeal box with lid
Colored paper
Heavy yarn
Old magazines
Scissors, glue

What You Do:

1. Glue colored paper around the oatmeal box.

2. Cut out pictures of your favorite foods from old magazines and glue them to your tote. While you are looking through the magazines, find the letters of your name, cut them out and glue them on too.

3. Make a small hole on each side of the oatmeal box near the top. Push the ends of a long piece of yarn through the holes and fasten. Put the lid on the box and your lunch tote is ready.

SANDWICH CONE

Tuck a lettuce leaf into a flat-bottomed ice cream cone, and fill with egg salad, tuna salad, or cottage cheese. Top with mandarin orange slices or cherries. Or try:

CARROT-RAISIN FILLING

Combine ½ cup each of raisins, shredded carrots, and cottage cheese. Add 1 Tbsp. mayonnaise and a dash of salt. Refrigerate for an hour to blend flavors. Makes enough for 4 cones.

TRAIL SNACK PAK

Combine assorted munchies (raisins, peanuts, dried fruit, cold cereal, popcorn, pretzels) in a small plastic bag and close with wire bag tie. Place the bag in the center of a large, colorful square of cloth, and tie the opposite corners together. The snack pack can be tied to your belt.

MILK AND HONEY TREAT

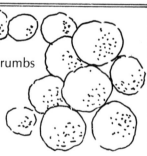

1¼ c. graham cracker crumbs
¼ c. sugar
½ tsp. cinnamon
½ c. peanut butter
⅓ c. honey
¼ c. powdered milk

Combine crumbs, sugar, and cinnamon. Stir in peanut butter and honey, and mix well. Roll into balls. Chill. Makes 2 dozen.

BASKETBALL RELAY

Put a wastebasket at the goal line. Each player dribbles the ball to the goal, puts it in the basket, takes it out, and dribbles back. The first team to finish wins.

RAINBOW TREASURE HUNT

Divide into two teams, and choose a captain for each. Make a list of things to hunt for, and give each team captain a copy of the list and a paper bag. If children cannot read, the list can be pictures instead of words. Set a time limit for everyone to return to the picnic area. The winner is the team which has found the most items on the list.

TEAM 1

TEAM 2

SCHOLAR'S RELAY

Give each team a book. Each player must carry it to the goal and back — but on his or her head. If the book drops, the player must pick it up and keep going.

119

SHAVUOT

Our homes and synagogues are filled with fresh flowers, as we welcome the spring harvest of the first fruits. Shavuot was the day the people of Israel received the Torah. Do you know all of the Ten Commandments? Because it is the end of the school year, many students celebrate confirmation.

WORDS TO KNOW

Shavuot — Feast of Weeks; celebrated seven weeks after Passover
Torah — the first five books of the Bible
Confirmation — graduation from religious school
Ten Commandments — the ten most important laws in the Torah

SHAVUOT

STAR OF DAVID

What You Need:

Six popsicle sticks
Construction paper
Glue, markers

What You Do:

1. Glue 3 popsicle sticks together to form a triangle. Repeat with 3 more sticks.

2. Glue the two triangles together to form a star. Decorate.

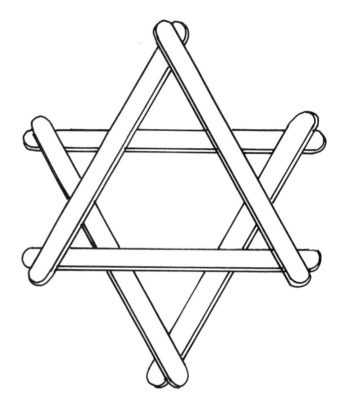

TEN COMMANDMENTS

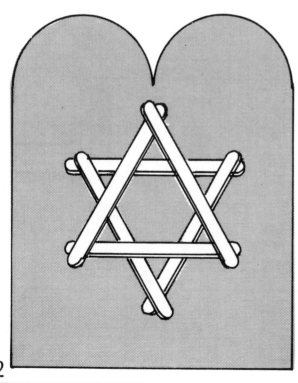

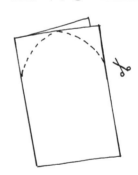

What You Do:

1. Make a Star of David as described above. Paint it and let it dry.

2. Fold a piece of colored paper in half. Cut off the corners as shown. Unfold.

3. Glue your star to the tablet and decorate.

What You Need:

Colored paper
White paper
Scissors, glue

What You Do:

TEN COMMANDMENTS:

1. Fold a piece of white paper in half. Cut a curve along the top two edges.

2. Fold the paper in half again. Cut five shapes on the long folded side.

3. Unfold and glue onto colored paper.

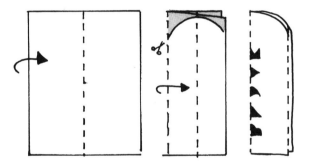

STAR OF DAVID:

1. Fold a circle of white paper in half and in half again. Then fold in each side to make an ice cream cone shape.

2. Cut off the bottom point at a slant. Cut out shapes along the folds on the sides and top.

3. Unfold and glue onto colored paper.

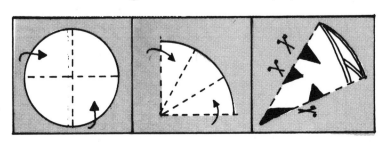

FLOWERS
FOR YOUR TABLE

Leaf

What You Need:

Cardboard
Small cardboard roll
Straws, muffin cups
Tissue paper, colored paper, fabric scraps
Glue, scissors, paint

What You Do:

1. To make the vase, cut out a circle larger than the bottom of the roll, and glue the roll to the circle. Dry completely. Decorate.

2. To make flowers, flatten one end of a long straw. Glue 2 muffin cups together with the straw in the middle. Glue tissue paper or fabric scraps in the center of each flower.

3. Cut out leaves (you may trace the shape above) and glue to the straws.

4. Make several different kinds of flowers and put them in your vase.

HARVEST BASKET

What You Need:

Egg carton lid
Colored paper
Black tissue paper
Scissors, glue, stapler, markers

What You Do:

1. Decorate the outside of an egg carton lid. Staple two strips of paper onto the lid for the handle. Put one strip across the long side and the other strip across the short side.

2. Draw and cut out large pieces of fruit from colored paper. Glue them in the basket. Make apples, bananas. pears, grapefruit, oranges, and grapes.

3. Look in a shoe box for black tissue paper. Cut and pinch small pieces to make dates and raisins. Glue them on top of the other fruit.

CONFIRMATION CAP

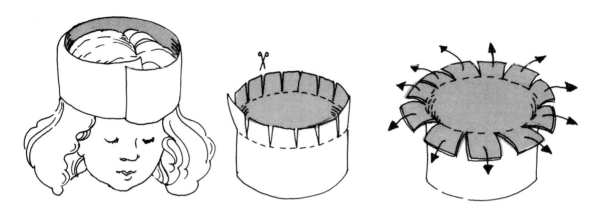

What You Do:

1. Measure a long strip of paper to fit your head. Glue the ends together. Cut slits one third of the way down all around the top of the headband. Fold the flaps outward.

2. Cut a square of paper larger than the headband. Put glue on the flaps of the headband and press them onto the paper square.

3. Make a tassle with blue and white yarn and fasten it to the center.

What You Need:

Construction paper
Paper fastener
Blue and white yarn
Scissors, glue

HOLIDAY SEWING CARDS

What You Need:

Plastic bottles or styrofoam trays
Yarn
Tape, markers, hole punch

What You Do:

1. Cut holiday symbols from plastic bottle or tray.

2. Punch holes around the edges of the symbols.

3. Cut a piece of yarn and wrap tape around one end to form a "needle." Knot the other end.

4. Sew your holiday cards. Decorate with markers.

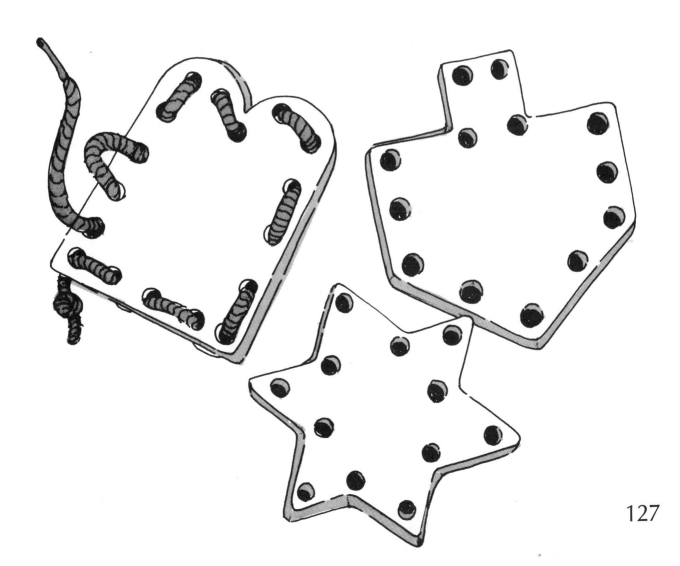

ABOUT THE AUTHOR

During her long career as a preschool teacher and director, Ruth Brinn guided young hearts, minds, and hands. Hundreds of children returned home from her classes clutching the projects in this book, beaming, ''Look what I made. . .all by myself.'' The beauty of Ruth's book is its simplicity. There are no hot stoves, hard-to-find materials, or complicated directions to discourage the eager young child.

Ruth continues to write and teach about Jewish holiday celebrations. She and her husband live in Sarasota, FL.

ABOUT THE ILLUSTRATOR

Katherine Janus Kahn, an illustrator and calligrapher, studied Fine Arts at the Bezalel School in Jerusalem and the University of Iowa. She has illustrated an impressive list of more than two dozen picture books, toddler board books, and activity books for young children, including *Alef Is One*, *A Family Haggadah*, *The Passover Parrot*, and *Shabbat, A Family Service*. She lives in Wheaton, MD with her husband David and son Robert.